Praise for *God Is My CEO*

"Surely, for the faithful, Julian's book must arrive as a comfort in corporate times, a balm in business, a printed sanctuary for souls strained in the modern workplace."

—CNN.com

"Larry Julian's God Is My CEO *is a more serious work, capturing some of the difficulty of combining Christianity and capitalism.*"

—Wall Street Journal

"Many leaders, whether newly indoctrinated to the world of business or veteran executives, will find tools for the trade in this excellent guidebook."

—Publishers Weekly

"Newcomers to the business world will find nuggets of gold in these pages and the more seasoned traveler will find an oasis where they can be rejuvenated."

—Stan Geyer, Former President and CEO, Fluoroware

"God Is My CEO *should be read by all CEOs or anyone in a leadership position. If your company is driven by mission rather than the bottom line, this book will strengthen your position.*"

—Anne Beiler, Founder and CEO, Auntie Anne's Hand-Rolled Soft Pretzels

"The practical approach of having CEOs give their answers to real-life situations is an extremely practical way to give advice. What's most important, however, is the biblical foundation which has been authenticated in the lives of the men and women highlighted in God Is My CEO."

—Wes Cantrell, Chairman and Former CEO, Lanier Worldwide, Inc.

"In challenging times, those leaders who can reach deep within themselves and draw upon an inner strength fortified by strong moral values and a depth of character—those leaders will be successful. God Is My CEO provides the guide to those values and that depth of character. It is a must-read for those who lead the efforts of others."

—General Charles C. Krulak (Ret.), 31st Commandant, U.S. Marine Corps; Chairman and CEO, MBNA Europe

"Unlike the countless leadership books on the market, this one will never be out of date, because the biblical principles offered in this book are timeless."

—Marc Belton, Executive Vice President, Global Strategy, Growth and Marketing Innovation, General Mills

"God Is My CEO is direct, on target, beautiful, and convincing. Excellent!"

—Zig Ziglar, Motivational Teacher, Author of See You at the Top

"Larry Julian has written a game plan to help all of us score a touchdown in life. Whether you are a football coach, self-employed, or chairman of the board, the principles in God Is My CEO can help you define the champion within."

—Dan Reeves, Former Head Coach, Atlanta Falcons

"Congratulations on God Is My CEO—it is a powerful and much needed book."

—George H. Gallup, Former Chairman, The George H. Gallup International Institute

"God Is My CEO is a gem of a book. It sure challenged me in my role as a leader and it will do the same for you. A powerful read."

—Pat Williams, Senior Vice Present, Orlando Magic

GOD

is my

CEO

——— 2nd Edition ———

GOD
is my
CEO

2nd Edition

Following God's Principles in a Bottom-Line World

Larry Julian

Avon, Massachusetts

Published by
Adams Media, a division of F+W Media, Inc.
57 Littlefield Street, Avon, MA 02322. U.S.A.
www.adamsmedia.com

ISBN 10: 1-4405-6517-1
ISBN 13: 978-1-4405-6517-5
eISBN 10: 1-4405-6518-X
eISBN 13: 978-1-4405-6518-2

Printed in the United States of America.

10 9 8 7 6 5 4 3 2 1

Library of Congress Cataloging-in-Publication Data

Julian, Larry
    God is my CEO: following God's principles in a bottom-line world / Larry Julian. -- 2nd Edition.
        pages cm
    Includes bibliographical references and index.
    ISBN-13: 978-1-4405-6517-5 (pb : alk. paper)
    ISBN-10: 1-4405-6517-1 (pb : alk. paper)
    ISBN-13: 978-1-4405-6518-2 (ebook)
    ISBN-10: 1-4405-6518-X (ebook)
    1. Businesspeople--Religious life. 2. Business--Religious aspects--Christianity. I. Title.
BV4596.B8J85 2014
248.8'8--dc23
                                                        2013044603

Many of the designations used by manufacturers and sellers to distinguish their product are claimed as trademarks. Where those designations appear in this book and F+W Media, Inc. was aware of a trademark claim, the designations have been printed with initial capital letters.

The *Life Application Study Bible: New International Edition* was used for biblical references throughout this book. Published by Tyndale House Publishers, Wheaton, Illinois, 1997.

Reprinted by permission. *The Hole in Our Gospel*, Richard Stearns, copyright 2010, Thomas Nelson Inc., Nashville, Tennessee. All rights reserved.

Reprinted by permission. *Love Works*, Richard Stearns, copyright 2012, Zondervan, Grand Rapids, Michigan. All rights reserved.

This book is available at quantity discounts for bulk purchases.
For information, please call 1-800-289-0963.

DEDICATION

To my Lord, Jesus Christ.
Thank you for the privilege of it all.

CONTENTS

Chapter 3

Courage / 68

Chapter 4

Patience / 83

Chapter 8

Love / 152

Chapter 9

Priorities / 179

CONTENTS

Conclusion

A Message of Hope / 259

Appendix

Your Personal Business Plan / 265

ACKNOWLEDGMENTS

Special thanks to my family, especially my wife, Sherri, and my children, Grace and Scott, who allow me to experience God's love every day. My heartfelt appreciation also goes out to Scott and Judy Hackett, Matt and Lolly Pisoni, Steve and Lesley Hackett, and my mom.

My gratitude runs deep to friends who inspire me by boldly living their faith in the business world: Dean Bachelor, Jay Bennett, Marc Belton, Ward Brehm, John Busacker, Jay Coughlan, Dennis Doyle, Gordy Engel, Art Erickson, David Frauenshuh, Os Guinness, Bill Hardman, Brad Hewitt, Ron James, Tad Piper, Al Prentice, Mike Sime, Rob Stevenson, and Phil Styrlund.

To the Leadership Roundtable members, past and present, who humbly seek to grow as leaders so they can honor God and serve others.

To Dan Rust for his Saturday morning insights, Steve Waller for supplying much-needed diversions, and to Jim Walter and John Zappala for their lifelong friendship.

To the National Prayer Breakfast Business Leader Forum team, who reflect the term "Jesus plus nothing" and who've taught me how to help diverse parties meet under the name and person of Jesus.

To the thirty-five leaders profiled in the pages herein who courageously and humbly shared their stories so they could inspire others to trust and follow a loving God in a bottom-line world.

To those whose daily presence has been lost but whose impact on my life will never be forgotten: Monty Sholund, Stan Geyer, Marty Sinacore, and my dad.

And finally, to my Lord Jesus Christ, thank you for bringing all these people into my life to help me grow closer to you, so that I might be an instrument for your noble purpose.

PREFACE

God designed you to work. Work was designed by God.

If these two statements are true, then one of the most important endeavors you can embrace is to bring your faith and work into harmony. The result is a life of meaning, purpose, satisfaction, and eternal significance.

A life whose work and faith hasn't been joined together becomes one of toil and drudgery. Days become filled with worry, frustration, and exhaustion.

To reconcile means to find a way of restoring two different ideas to harmony. Your work. Your faith. Two different ideas. Finding a way to restore them to harmony is the purpose of this book. Together, we explore, *How do I join my faith and work?*

God Is My CEO was first written more than a decade ago to help answer this question.

In the years in between that first edition and this one, I've been moved by how God has used the concepts in this book to impact lives. Many readers have shared heartwarming stories of the meaning and purpose they've discovered:

- The CEO of a retailer in China who found renewed purpose to align her calling and her talents
- A nurse who took his skills and created a hospice organization based on the principles of love, mercy, and compassion
- A college graduate who, discouraged by her failure to secure a job, discovered God's plan for her life in between the lines of the *God Is My CEO* business plan

- The stay-at-home mom who, following the loss of her daughter to a rare disease, was inspired to become an author and advocate for others in the same situation
- The human resources executive who was able to reconcile her faith with her company's HR policies, giving her a renewed sense of purpose and enthusiasm for her job
- The sales manager who determined that the most effective way to change his sales philosophy from "what can I get?" to "how can I give?" was to start his own business

Some of you represent a new generation of leaders with an incredible array of gifts, talents, and energy levels who are seeking ways to integrate your faith and passion into your work.

Some of you are closer to my age. Understanding the brevity of life, you seek significance in the second half of your life. Your gray hair represents a wealth of gifts, talents, and experiences. Some of you find yourselves in your prime leadership years. Others may find your gifts and experiences to be undervalued and unappreciated. Still others are looking to define calling in the second half of life.

Regardless of where you are in your career, the message is the same: Your work is important to God. Your calling lasts a lifetime. Your work serves a purpose beyond yourself. And the significance of your work is eternal.

This revised *God Is My CEO* is designed to take your work and faith to another level. You will grow as a leader at work, at home, and in your community. The core of the book remains the encouraging stories of contemporary leaders—stories that will inspire you to live out your faith and values in today's demanding business world. In addition to these practical examples, we've added four important features.

1. In the new "Timeless Wisdom from Twenty Leaders" section, twenty leaders have shared parts of their personal stories. Based on the concept alone, I had great hopes for this section. The result, however, far exceeds my expectations. The depth of insight in these twenty messages will stimulate your thinking and influence who you are as a leader.

2. The new chapter on redemption, Chapter 10, will renew your hope in a God of second chances. If you feel mired in failure and defeat, these stories will provide hope and encouragement. More importantly, you'll discover that failure can be an important stepping-stone toward success and significance.

3. A new chapter on love, Chapter 8, demonstrates that you don't have to choose between love and the bottom line. Leading with love helps build healthy relationships amongst stakeholders, aligns employees' personal values with their work values, and increases the probability of profitability and sustainability. In short, leading with love is good for business.

4. Finally, we've added a link to my website, *www.larryjulian .com*, to help you put your knowledge into practical action. In addition to other training material, free resources available to you include a Leader's Guide to help you create and facilitate a twelve-week *God Is My CEO* discussion group. Connecting with a small group of like-minded peers in a trusting environment is a proven vehicle to help you succeed and grow personally, professionally, and spiritually.

So let's get to it. I pray the words and stories that follow will be a catalyst to helping you discover greater meaning and purpose in your work, and that you would have the courage to embrace this life-changing journey toward finding and fulfilling God's call upon your life.

Introduction

The Clash of Two Worlds

Issue:

We are led by bottom-line pressures.

For a man is a slave to whatever has mastered him.

—2 Peter 2:19

I was asked to conduct a leadership program for a group of San Francisco sales executives. As part of my preparation, the leader asked me to weave in a module on stress management. During the program, I discovered that the group was on the brink of a collective nervous breakdown. They were under relentless pressure to produce results and felt as if they were strapped to a treadmill whose speed kept increasing.

I wanted to help them find the root cause of their situation. The sales executives, however, only wanted me to equip them with skills so that I could help them run their treadmill faster and better. In essence, they wanted me to teach them how to go down the wrong path more efficiently.

The bottom line had become their god. It was insatiable. No matter how hard they worked, it was never enough, nor would it ever be enough. These executives were talented, intelligent, capable people who, somewhere along the way, lost focus on what is truly meaningful and important. They had become slaves to bottom-line pressure and, as a result, became professionally ineffective and personally burnt out.

Solution:

Let God lead.

Trust in the Lord with all your heart, and lean not on your own understanding. In all your ways acknowledge Him, and He shall make your paths straight.

—Proverbs 3:5–6

In my work as a management consultant, I find people in all positions, from CEOs to line employees, wrestling with challenging dilemmas and trying to make sense out of situations that have no simple solutions. These are talented people who want to make a difference, but who are stuck in a quagmire of urgent deadlines, unrealistic expectations, and politics.

There are times when critical business decisions have no correct answer and can only be made with a leap of faith by the leader alone. The solution is to trust God's principles, which will help us be effective and significant leaders in the midst of a pressured and demanding world.

A ship that turns its direction by one degree will alter its course by hundreds of miles. In the same way, your decision to trust in God will have a significant impact on the direction in which you're headed. The more you trust, the more freedom you'll gain from the shackles of the urgent, bottom-line pressures that enslave you. The more freedom you have, the more significant a leader you'll become.

Biblical Principles versus Bottom-Line Demands

At our very core, we want meaning and purpose in our work. We are looking for appreciation and affirmation for our contributions, satisfying answers to ethical dilemmas, clarity and direction in the midst of confusion, and a sense of fulfillment. This common theme crosses every layer of management and extends across races, nationalities, religions, and genders.

We usually want to do the right thing but often succumb to the short-term, bottom-line demands of daily business life. While we are encouraged to follow God on Sunday, we are not supported to make the right ethical decisions in the trenches on Monday through Friday.

This paradigm has demanded that we operate in two separate worlds: a deeply personal, private, spiritual world and a very public, demanding, competitive business world. For the most part, these two worlds clash in their values, beliefs, and principles, and we are caught in the middle.

This separation between a true longing for meaning in the workplace and the demand to help our employers survive and thrive creates a tremendous internal dilemma. The elements of this dilemma are shown on the following page.

Business Principles versus God's Principles

Unwritten Business Rules	God's Principles
• Achieve results	• Serve a purpose
• What can I get?	• How can I give?
• Success = dollars	• Significance = people
• Work to please people	• Work to please God
• Fear of the unknown	• Living with hope
• Leadership is being first	• Leadership is being last
• Take charge; surrender means defeat	• Let go; surrender means victory
• The end justifies the means. Get to the outcome regardless of how you accomplish it.	• The means justify the end. Do the right thing regardless of the outcome.
• Short-term gain	• Long-term legacy
• Slave to the urgent	• Freedom of choice
• You can never produce enough	• Unconditional love

We commonly view this dilemma as an internal struggle between right and wrong. We seem to be presented with a disturbing choice: Either we embrace bottom-line success and turn from God, or we accept and live by God's principles and suffer whatever negative business consequences come our way. We are challenged by questions like "Can I do what's right and be successful in a competitive, bottom-line world?" and "Can I be both ethical and profitable?"

If you trust in God's principles, have the courage to live them, and have the patience to wait on His timing, then I believe the answer to these questions is "Yes." Biblical principles and bottom-line success are not opposites. Yes, *you can* do what's right and be successful.

Yes, *you can* be both ethical and profitable. And yes, *you can* honor God, serve others, and fulfill your professional obligations.

God did not call us to be victims of circumstance. He calls us to grow closer to Him by courageously working through our dilemmas. He wants us to prosper, to be valuable leaders, and to serve as models to help others.

God's design of leadership has a solid foundation and is built to grow stronger over time *in the midst of external pressure*. This leadership model utilizes time and pressure to yield wisdom, growth in character, and maximum productivity.

When you integrate God's principles with your unique talents, skills, and character, you create a powerful partnership for being successful in the world without becoming of the world. As a result, your *challenges and dilemmas strengthen you* to become the successful and significant leader God intended you to be.

God's wisdom, your spiritual core, provides your source of strength, purpose, and direction, and balances and leverages your skills and abilities. **Your character** is the aggregate sum of who you are as you courageously follow through and do what's right over time. **Your productivity** is the legacy you leave behind.

Worldly and Godly Leadership: The Differences

Worldly Leaders	Godly Leaders
• Pressure weakens them.	• Pressure strengthens them.
• Prioritizing profits over principles reduces their value over time.	• Prioritizing principles over profits enhances their value over time.
• Their character weakens over time.	• Their character strengthens over time.
• They produce nothing other than bottom-line results.	• They produce a legacy in addition to bottom-line results.

At the core of the quest for meaningful work lies a clash between two masters who demand to be first in your heart and mind. In the end, you have to choose.

Your future is determined by what you believe and do. Every one of your beliefs generates behavior, and every behavior has a consequence. Ultimately, *you become what you believe and do every day*. As Charles Reade stated, "Sow an act and you reap a habit; sow a habit and you reap a character; sow a character and you reap a destiny."

It's essential to understand the impact of your beliefs and actions, because they shape your future. What are the beliefs that drive your business decisions? Does your faith define who you are at work, or do the business rules define who you are? Are you on the right path?

In His wisdom, God provides us with the freedom to think and choose. This book isn't about preaching religion, nor is it a debate about what is right or wrong. Rather, this book is about helping you make the right choices in challenging circumstances. Your dilemmas are natural stepping-stones on your path to success. The goal of this book is not to provide you with prepackaged solutions to your dilemmas but to help you work through the process of solving them yourself.

Very simply, this book is intended to help you reflect on your beliefs and to seek God to equip and encourage you to do the right thing under pressure. This process will put you on the most important and meaningful path in your life.

How This Book Will Help You

In order for you to become a successful godly leader, you should be regularly developing and integrating these two areas:

1. The outer development of your God-given talents and skills
2. The inner development of your spiritual core

This development occurs as a result of the wholehearted pursuit and practice of God's principles.

Thousands of leaders have great external leadership skills but no inner character. There are also many people of great character who do not have the necessary leadership skills. This book will help you combine these two elements to help you become a successful and significant leader.

Throughout the book, you will reflect upon and respond to what is most important in your life and business rather than react and do the things you're pressured to do. You can reflect on God's principles and use them as potential solutions to difficult and confusing business issues.

To accomplish this, you'll need to rise above superficial business pressures to gain a bigger perspective. We'll explore the ten most common issues facing business people today and apply God's principles to these dilemmas. You can make the right choices and become the successful and significant person God has intended you to be.

Each chapter will do three things for you:

1. Help you gain ideas and encouragement from the real-life stories of twenty leaders who've faced the same challenges
2. Share God's principles as an alternative way to help you make wise decisions in the midst of challenging circumstances
3. Provide a simple and practical Discussion Guide to help focus your thoughts and move you forward with a sense of purpose

A Final Thought on Your Quest

This book is designed to help you make two important connections. First, it will help you connect with other leaders in a safe, nonthreatening way to share ideas and insights on being a godly leader. (For more information on establishing a small group, visit *www.larryjulian.com.*) Second, and most important, it will help you connect with God in your workplace. As you move through this book, remember why you're taking on this effort. God loves you, has a purpose for your life, and wants you to succeed. As you focus on your spiritual growth, keep in mind that you are being prepared for significant rewards far beyond what you can possibly imagine. Enjoy the journey.

DISCUSSION GUIDE

1. Describe the risks and rewards of being a godly leader in a bottom-line world.
2. Review the chart listing the unwritten business rules and God's principles. What beliefs (from either side of the chart) currently drive your business decisions?
3. What erroneous belief enslaves you the most and hinders your effectiveness?
4. What specific steps can you take to eliminate or reduce this erroneous belief?
5. Which principle means the most to you, and why?
6. What specific steps can you take to live by that principle?

1

Purpose

From earning a living to serving a purpose

In all things God works for the good of those who love Him, who have been called according to His purpose.
—Romans 8:28

Issue:

How do I find meaning and purpose in my work?

Helping an executive team clarify their mission statement, I began by asking the fundamental question, "What is the purpose of your company?" Instead of answering the question, team members focused on developing words and phrases that would sound appealing to their shareholders, customers, and employees. They spent hours wordsmithing phrases such as "maximizing profitability," "world-class service," and "our employees are our greatest asset." Hours had been spent on the words, but there was no meaning behind them.

It was almost noon when the company's president arrived. He walked into the room and glanced at the flip chart with the carefully crafted phrases. Turning to the group, he said, "Let me bottom-line this. Our purpose is to increase revenue 15 percent and we have eleven months and ten days to do it."

Employees look for meaning and purpose in their work, yet in reality, the pressure for company profitability often takes precedence over employee and company meaning and purpose. Is there more to work than earning a paycheck? The answer is yes, but we need to look in the mirror and honestly ask ourselves, "What is our priority? What purpose do we serve? To what end?"

Solution:

Find God's calling and find your purpose.

God wants us to be successful. Not only does He plant the motivation in our hearts but He also gives us an intrinsic desire to contribute, add value, and connect with others in some meaningful endeavor. Finding meaning and purpose in our work is the key to both personal fulfillment and professional success.

Our purpose drives everything else: what we do, how we do it, and for whom we work. It gives us a reason to get out of bed in the morning and gives direction to our days.

In this chapter, we'll learn how Bill George's journey led him to become CEO of Medtronic, providing him with personal fulfillment after a thirty-year search. Then, we'll learn from Bill Pollard, chairman emeritus of The ServiceMaster Company, whose brandnames include Merry Maids and Terminix, among others, how creating meaning and purpose for employees is the key to his organization's success. In both cases, we'll see how turning to God to find meaning and purpose can lead to both personal and professional fulfillment and success.

What's the key to their impressive track records in growth and profitability? In both companies, purpose takes precedence over profitability. Shareholder profits and long-term growth have been the *result* of their mission, not the mission itself.

BILL GEORGE
"Finding Your Way Home"

Whether in an entry-level position or CEO, people long to find meaning and purpose in their work. For Bill George, former CEO of Medtronic, the world's largest therapeutic medical technology company and supplier of more than half the pacemakers implanted throughout the world, it was a thirty-year journey through a maze of challenges, opportunities, and some disillusionment. Only then did he come to the place he could call home, a place to fulfill his calling and make a difference—God's way.

Grace Cathedral on San Francisco's Nob Hill is a special place for Bill and his wife Penny. On the grounds, there's a beautiful labyrinth, an intricate maze that winds its way to the center. Trying to figure out the right path can be frustrating. There are roadblocks and choices between left and right turns before getting to the center. Bill sees the journey through the maze as a metaphor for the process of finding meaning and purpose in his life.

Like the choices in the labyrinth, Bill's main conflict has been trying to discern between God's calling for his life, and his ego. "Since I was a teenager," says Bill, "I felt that God had a mission for my life. I felt that my mission was to become the head of a major corporation so I could influence other leaders by the way I conducted myself. Making a difference was a very important drive in my life. Sometimes I got confused as to who I was making a difference for. Many times, making a difference translated into ego, recognition, and power. I had to constantly challenge myself by asking, 'For whom?' and 'For what purpose?'"

Bill's quest to fulfill his calling was very much on track. However, the sense of fulfillment that comes from being aligned with God's calling was drifting away. From a business perspective, Bill was moving quickly toward becoming CEO of a major corporation. His resume included Harvard Business School and president of Litton Microwave. By 1983, he was one of the top five executives at Honeywell. As Bill rose to the top of Honeywell, he received many job offers from around the country. One of the pursuing companies was a small, Minneapolis-based company called Medtronic. Medtronic first approached Bill to become their president and CEO in 1978, again in 1986, and yet again in 1988.

Bill repeatedly turned down each offer because he didn't think Medtronic fit into his calling. His ego told him that a $750 million company wasn't enough to satisfy his ambitions because he was already running a $2 billion organization with three times the number of employees.

Though Bill knew of Medtronic's fine reputation, he turned down each offer as he single-mindedly moved toward his goal. He felt he was getting closer and closer to what he thought was his calling, but in reality, he was drifting farther and farther away. He explains, "I was trying to change the culture at Honeywell to reflect my values and philosophy. In reality, the culture at Honeywell was changing me. I realized that I was acting out a role designed to get ahead."

Bill was in charge of nine divisions, and eight of them were out of town. As time went on, he became more intense and felt more uptight. The harder he ran, the faster the treadmill sped up—but he wasn't going anywhere. It became clear to Bill that he was running so hard he couldn't stop long enough to hear God's voice.

For many years, Bill continued to pursue his goal to be CEO of a major corporation, believing that was the platform he needed to carry out God's call. In the fall of 1988, he finally hit the wall. One day, as he was driving home from work, Bill looked around at the beauty of the community where he lived. The fall foliage was starting to come out in the grand maple-lined parkway that surrounded Lake of the Isles. This beautiful picture reminded him of a special retreat weekend in which he had participated.

"I realized back then that I had compartmentalized my life into work, home, spiritual, and community," Bill relates. "At that retreat, I knocked down the walls, making one big room. It gave me the freedom to be who I am. I realized that I let the world compartmentalize me back then, and now I was allowing it to happen to me again. When I saw the beauty of Lake of the Isles, it represented the open room. That vision made me stop and think, 'Here's this wonderful life I have been blessed with and I'm wandering in the desert. Where am I going?'"

Bill realized that his current job situation was changing him in ways he didn't like. "I might become CEO of Honeywell or I could wind up taking a job as CEO of some undefined company in some unknown community just to satisfy my ego's ambitions, all of which would force my wife, Penny, to quit her job and cause our sons to change schools just as they were coming into their high school years at a school they both loved. And why? To satisfy my ego to be CEO of a major corporation? To what end?"

That evening, Bill talked to Penny about his new insights, and the two of them prayed together. He openly questioned if it was important to be CEO of a megacorporation. For the first time he saw clearly that such things were of little or no importance. Bill refocused on what was important: his marriage to Penny, their family, their friends, their ties to the community, and the opportunity to make a big difference in a smaller company with great potential.

Bill explains, "Nothing against Honeywell, but I needed a change in venue and a change in outlook. I needed time to listen, really listen to the inner voice that is the Lord's calling. I asked a close friend to call Win Wallin, then CEO of Medtronic, and tell him that I was available after all if the job was still open. I was fortunate to find that the position was still available."

Earl Bakken, the founder of Medtronic, met with Bill in Phoenix while he was on a business trip. Earl had taken the time to fly from Hawaii to meet with the potential new CEO. Talking with Earl, Bill had the sense that he had found the place where his calling could be realized. "It was an immediate values fit," Bill recalls. "This was meant to be. I was fortunate enough to get the job. The moment I stepped through the doors at Medtronic, I knew I had come home."

Looking back, Bill realizes that Medtronic was where he belonged all along. At Medtronic he could openly express and share his values, dreams, hopes, and fears. Through Medtronic's unique mission, written in 1960 by founder Earl Bakken, Bill could help carry out God's call to restore people to full life and health, and he can act as an ethical servant leader. "The 'call' had been there since 1978, yet I hadn't heard it. More precisely, I wasn't prepared to receive it. I had to go through the maze before I came to the center, which was God's call, not mine."

Since 2004, Bill has taught leadership as a professor of management practice at Harvard Business School. He's also authored four bestselling books: *7 Lessons for Leading in Crisis*, *True North*, *Finding Your True North*, and *Authentic Leadership*. Since leaving Medtronic, Bill has also served as a director for several corporations and nonprofit organizations.

Bill's eyes light up when he talks about Medtronic's mission. "The previous companies I worked for had good values, but we couldn't discuss the things that were meaningful in our lives. At Medtronic, people talked about their faith and values all the time. Open discussion was encouraged because talking about values creates bonding to others and to a meaningful common purpose. The employees at Medtronic are committed to our mission of restoring people to full life and health."

Bill explains that Medtronic has been successful because it's a mission-driven company. Medtronic isn't in the business of maximizing shareholder value. They're in the business of maximizing the value of the patients they serve. "That's what motivates our people!" says Bill. "My entire work experience leads me to believe that people want to find genuine meaning in their work, to believe that they are working for a higher purpose, to believe that they can make a difference in the lives of others. At Medtronic, if we serve our patients well, we will do very well and increase our shareholder value a lot. If our 23,000 employees are motivated by the same common purpose, we will be very successful."

Medtronic's leaders work hard to achieve an open dialogue with employees. They do this through several vehicles: informal employee breakfasts; new employee sessions with the founder, Earl Bakken, or the CEO; a holiday party; all-employee meetings; and a wide range of one-on-one sessions. For example, the company personally gives a special medallion that represents Medtronic's mission to every employee who joins the company. Bill explains, "They say to the employee, 'This medallion can only be given to a Medtronic employee. By accepting this medallion, you are making a commitment to give your best effort to restoring people to full life and health.' This simple gesture is very meaningful to our employees. It tells them that their work has meaning—it goes beyond just earning a buck."

Bill finds that, almost without exception, Medtronic employees are motivated to achieve the unsurpassed quality called for in the Medtronic mission. They look for meaning in their work, a meaning that is usually underpinned by a solid spiritual base. The company has a wide range of belief systems represented: Christians, Jews, Muslims, Hindus, Buddhists, and many who have no established faith at all. But there's a sense that they're on a common path, searching for deeper meaning and fulfillment in their work, for the ability to help and serve others.

Medtronic celebrates its mission at the annual holiday party, a tradition for the past forty years. Every year six people come in to share how Medtronic's employees have made a difference in their lives. Even though nine million people benefited from Medtronic technologies in 2012, for example, it's more personalized when one person tells the employees, "If it weren't for you, my two-year-old daughter wouldn't be here today. You saved her life."

Just listening to Bill convinced me that Medtronic employees are truly motivated by serving a higher purpose. Although somewhat reserved at the beginning of our interview, Bill was passionate when he spoke of the people at Medtronic. After a brief pause, I asked him, "What about you? When you worked for the company, how did you redefine your calling to find fulfillment?"

Bill jumped up and walked over to his desk. I was startled, thinking perhaps I had offended him and the interview was over. Then I noticed the huge grin on his face as he walked back to the table. Bill handed me a framed picture.

"This is T.J. When I first started at Medtronic, the company was faced with a division that was losing a lot of money—we were losing approximately five million dollars a year and had already lost about thirty-five to forty million dollars. We were ready to shut the division down. But then I met T.J. at my first holiday party." Bill explained that T.J. had cerebral palsy and had come to the holiday party to share what it meant to be functional, thanks to the drug pump that this "losing" division manufactured. T.J. became a real-life example of Medtronic's mission. Bill found it easy to relate to him because T.J. was the same age as his own son. T.J.'s story enlivened everyone. Bill says, "After the holiday party, we all got together with one goal in mind: How can we make this division work? We found a way to restructure the division, and today it is one of our most profitable divisions." No doubt, Bill's passion for helping people has empowered his employees to meet such challenges.

One could argue that Bill has already fulfilled his calling. He's been CEO of the world's preeminent medical technology company. Medtronic's revenues have grown to $16.5 billion and earnings per share have jumped to $3.70 on an average share price of $57.16 (as of 2014). All of this sounds impressive, but I had to research Medtronic's financial results for myself because Bill never mentioned them during our interview. He was too busy talking about T.J., particularly T.J.'s accomplishments since they had met in 1989. "I am so proud of T.J. He's doing extremely well. He's married, has graduated from college, has a good job, and is leading a very successful life."

Finally, I asked Bill if he thought he had achieved his original mission now that he has been the head of a major corporation. Bill responded, "I don't think I had the influence on CEOs the way I originally planned. However, I now feel like I'm fulfilling my mission, as I'm able to influence many more people, of all ages, than I ever dreamed possible and understand what it means to serve others through your business."

It was evident observing the joy on Bill's face as he talked about his family, Medtronic's employees, and T.J., that Bill had found his calling. It's the same joy we get when we come home.

C. WILLIAM POLLARD
"Serving a Higher Purpose and Making Money"

How does one honor God, allow employees to find meaning and purpose in their work, and run a profitable business? One could easily argue that the reason for being in business is to make money and that while finding meaning and purpose is a noble pursuit, maximizing shareholder profits is the priority. The ServiceMaster Company, a nationwide service business, is very profitable, but to the 51,000 employees who serve more than eight million customers in thirty countries, their work provides much more than just profits.

Imagine a shareholder walking through ServiceMaster's lobby at their Downers Grove, Illinois, headquarters and seeing a marble statue of Christ washing the feet of a disciple. Beyond the statue is a wall that stands eighteen feet tall and stretches ninety feet across. Engraved in the wall are these four statements that constitute the company's objectives:

> To honor God in all we do
> To help people develop
> To pursue excellence
> To grow profitably

Clearly, these are unusual statements for a publicly held company. We could, in fact, say they are controversial. How does Bill Pollard, chairman emeritus of ServiceMaster, explain to shareholders that ServiceMaster's mission to serve God takes a higher priority than profits?

In his insightful book, *The Soul of the Firm*, Bill Pollard describes how this question was posed at one of ServiceMaster's shareholder meetings. A shareholder, while praising Service-Master for its profit performance, made the following statement: "While I firmly support the right of an individual to his religious convictions and pursuits, I totally fail to appreciate the concept that ServiceMaster is, in fact, a vehicle for the work of God. The multiple references to this effect, in my opinion, do not belong in the annual business report. To interpret a service for profit (which is what ServiceMaster does) as the work of God is an incredible presumption. Furthermore, to make a profit is not a sin. I urge that next year's business report be confined to just that—business."[1]

Bill Pollard disagrees. Not only does he believe that God belongs in the business world; he believes that helping employees find meaning and purpose at work is the key to his organization's success. "God and business do mix," says Bill, "and profit is a standard for determining the effectiveness of our combined efforts. For us, the common link between God and profit is people. But we live and work in a diverse and pluralistic society, and some people may either question the existence of God or have different definitions for God. That is why at ServiceMaster we never allowed religion or the lack thereof to become a basis for exclusion or how we treated each other professionally or personally. At the same time, I believe the work environment need not be emasculated to a neutrality of no belief."[2]

The leaders at ServiceMaster believe that God has given each employee dignity, worth, potential, and freedom to choose. The goal is to build a firm that begins with God and accepts and develops the different people He created. In fact, it has been the key to ServiceMaster's success. This simple truth of recognizing the potential, dignity, and worth of the individual has been one of the most important factors in the success and growth of their business.

Bill George showed how saving lives adds meaning and purpose to each Medtronic employee's work. But how does an organization like ServiceMaster recognize and develop the potential, dignity, and worth of an employee who performs mundane tasks like mopping floors? Part of the answer is in leadership's role in providing dignity and respect.

Bill Pollard himself made a meaningful connection with ServiceMaster. A college administrator, professor, and lawyer, Bill was at a point in his life where change was imminent. He found himself faced with two very different career paths. He had an offer to become partner of a major law firm and an offer for a senior management position at ServiceMaster. The position at the law firm made more sense; it was a job he was comfortable doing and it offered a better financial package. The ServiceMaster opportunity was more of an unknown that would lead Bill into uncharted waters. However, Bill was intrigued by Service-Master's mission. He shared its values and saw an opportunity to pursue a meaningful mission and to learn more about himself and others. With a desire to learn the true meaning of service and servant leadership, Bill took a leap of faith and accepted the position at ServiceMaster.

He immediately understood and connected with employees' viewpoints. In one of ServiceMaster's programs, We Serve Day, every leader in the organization has the opportunity to participate in directly serving the customer. As part of Bill's training, he had to perform tasks that front-line service employees perform every day. He was assigned to work with the housekeeping team at Lutheran General Hospital cleaning corridors, patient rooms, and bathrooms. One special incident helped him understand the principles of dignity and worth and how these principles translate to employee meaning and purpose.

Bill, then chairman and CEO, was working in a busy hospital corridor. He was getting ready to mop the floor and people were busy coming and going. Suddenly a woman stopped and asked him, "Aren't you Bill Pollard?" He told her he was. The woman then introduced herself as a distant relative of his wife. She looked at Bill and his mop, and then shook her head. "Aren't you a lawyer?" she asked. Bill responded that he had a new job. The woman seemed embarrassed and leaned toward Bill, whispering, "Is everything all right at home?"[3]

This incident gave Bill tremendous insight, and ServiceMaster's mission came to life. Not only did he gain valuable insight into the work of ServiceMaster's employees; he was able to define what servant leadership is and how it describes the role of leadership at ServiceMaster.

At ServiceMaster, Bill believes that leadership begins with their objectives: to honor God in all they do, to help people develop, to pursue excellence, and to grow profitably. He explains, "In John 13 we read the story of how Jesus took a towel and a basin of water and washed the disciples' feet. In so doing, He taught his disciples that no leader is greater than the people he leads, and that even the humblest of tasks are worthy of the leader to do. Thus our role and obligation as leaders involves more than what a person does on the job. We must also be involved in what that person is becoming and how the work environment is contributing to the process."[4]

The mindset that people are primary is what sets ServiceMaster apart. ServiceMaster is not a manufacturing company; it is a service organization, employing people who serve. Bill feels that how well employees serve depends on how they are motivated, respected, and trained. "It is not just what we are doing, but what we are becoming in the process that gives us our distinct value and is uniquely human," he explains. "Every firm should be able to articulate a mission that reaches beyond the task and provides a hope that the efforts and activities of its people are adding up to something significant—so significant, in fact, that even more can be accomplished than is expected."[5]

GOD IS MY CEO

Servant leadership is an important part of helping employees find meaning and purpose at work, but how do employees make that meaningful connection? Put bluntly, how does an employee find meaning and purpose in cleaning a toilet?

Bill answered the question by speaking about Shirley. Shirley is a housekeeper in a 250-bed community hospital. That isn't what makes her different. She's different from other housekeepers because, after fifteen years, she was still excited about her work. Shirley had seen some changes. She had been moved from floor to floor. The chemicals, mop, and housekeeper's cart had been improved so she actually cleaned more rooms per day than she did five years previously. But some things never change. The bathrooms and toilets were still germ-ridden; the dirt on floors had to be mopped up; patients still spilled things; and some doctors still treated "the help" like lepers. But Shirley kept humming away. Why?

It all comes down to ServiceMaster's view of the work they do. Bill explains, "When Shirley sees her task as extending service to the patient in the bed, and herself as an integral part of supporting the work of the doctors and nurses, she has a cause—a cause that involves the health and welfare of others. She came to us, no doubt, merely looking for a job, but she brought to us an unlocked potential and desire to accomplish something significant. She recently confirmed the importance of her cause when she told me, 'If we don't clean with a quality effort, we can't keep the doctors and nurses in business; we can't accommodate patients. This place would be *closed* if we didn't have housekeeping.'"[6]

Shirley's story helps clarify how every employee, no matter how mundane his or her task, can find meaning in it, can contribute value to his or her organization, and can serve a higher purpose, in addition to earning a paycheck.

But how does ServiceMaster's commitment to helping employees find meaning and purpose translate into profitability? Bill tells us that their goal is to train, to equip, and to motivate people to

44

be more effective at work. He believes that if a person has clear direction and a real reason to serve, then that employee is more dependable and responsive to meet, solve, and exceed customers' expectations.

"Where do you begin when you are faced with starting a $24.4 million contract in a large city school system?" Bill asks as an example. "Morale is low. More than 14,000 windows are broken in 161 schools. Racial tensions, insecurity among union leaders, and a high rate of absenteeism complicate your task. You've promised a turnaround. The school board members have their necks on the line for hiring an outside contractor, and they want results yesterday!"[7] His answer shouldn't surprise us.

"You begin with people. At the first meeting we had with the employees, we provided light refreshments. Everyone came to the meeting and listened to our presentation, but nobody took the food. After the meeting, we discovered why: They didn't realize the food was for them. They had never been asked to participate in a meeting where food or service was provided for them."[8]

That was just the beginning. The leaders of ServiceMaster treated each worker with dignity and respect. Before long, the same workers who had felt so badly about their jobs began to respond with enthusiasm. Three months later, all of the broken windows had been repaired, the air conditioning (which some teachers didn't even know existed) was working again, and the entire look of the grounds changed from unkempt pastures of weeds to well-trimmed and flowered yards.

When the contract's anniversary date came, it was time to assess and recognize the progress. The city's newspaper ran a front-page story that lauded the improvements. School principals stated that ServiceMaster had helped improve communications within schools and had paved the way to organizing the custodial, maintenance, and grounds departments so they could be more responsive to the needs of school personnel. ServiceMaster went beyond the customer's expectations while saving the school district more than $3 million. Most surprising of all, ServiceMaster did it with *the same people who had been there before*. What happened? Bill explains, "The difference began with the way we treated them as people. They already had the dignity and potential. All we needed to do was to unlock that potential and provide training, direction, and recognition. It all goes back to our objectives and how we view people."[9]

ServiceMaster proves that the intangibles of respect, dignity, and service can contribute to the tangibles of profits and growth. In a world with constant change, economic slumps, and revolving management theories, ServiceMaster has demonstrated stellar growth and profitability with twenty years of record growth.

As Bill Pollard clarifies, "The objectives of our firm are not just carved in stone on the lobby wall. You can see them working every day in the lives of our people."[10] ServiceMaster demonstrates that providing meaning and purpose to employees not only honors God; it's good business.

CONCLUSION

Bill George and Bill Pollard acknowledge that finding meaning and purpose at work is a journey. Bill George described the journey as similar to going through a maze. You can't see the final destination; it's a matter of moving forward, trusting that God is leading you according to His purpose.

God never promised a straight path to success. Most likely, it's a maze filled with obstacles of all kinds. The question for each of us is whether we allow the obstacles to deter us or whether we move forward in spite of them. To move in the direction of the sun, a plant will go around obstacles until it blooms into a spectacular flower. The plant's purpose is to reach toward the sun.

Like the flower, a clear understanding of our purpose will enable us to move around, jump over, or break through our obstacles and bloom in our work settings.

God *is* leading us. The knowledge that we live our life with God's help provides the confidence, conviction, and focus that will move us forward regardless of circumstances. We can begin to understand that we have been called to meaningful work that far transcends any present job description. God did not call us to work the majority of our lives just to survive, earning a paycheck and existing from weekend to weekend. God created each person for specific reasons, tasks, and purposes, and He equipped each one of us with the perfect combination of talents, skills, and abilities required to find fulfillment for our lives.

Teaching about money, Jesus stated, "No one can serve two masters. Either he will hate the one and love the other or he will be devoted to the one and despise the other. You cannot serve both God and money." His underlying principle was about priorities. Our priority determines our course and measures our progress.

Jesus never said that money or financial success was wrong. He did say that prioritizing money over God is wrong. There is a greater purpose in our work beyond just making money, whether for ourselves or our corporations.

The organization whose purpose was to grow by 15 percent let its desire for profits diminish the primary purpose of its business. As business decisions subtly communicate to customers and employees that profit is more valuable than customer satisfaction and employee worth, the business will ultimately suffer the consequences of its priorities.

Those of us who are leaders of an organization should work to create a mission in which our organization's purpose is more than just making money. We can trust that serving a higher purpose will lead to business success. As we learned from ServiceMaster, creating an environment that provides dignity and respect and allowing employees to find meaning and purpose in their work will cause those employees to bloom gloriously. As we saw with Medtronic, the more we communicate the mission in terms the employee can relate to (such as Medtronic's holiday parties), the more motivated the employee is. In both case studies, all stakeholders, including company shareholders, customers, and employees, understood the higher priority and purpose of the organization.

We can't minimize the struggle we may have in finding meaning and purpose in our work. Here are three suggestions to help us.

1. **Find a Home**

   It's important to find the environment that unleashes your talents and recognizes your contributions. The environment that is right for one person may not be right for another. Both Bill Pollard and Bill George found the right organizations in which to bloom. We are also being called to bloom—not only for our benefit, but for the benefit of others. This may mean leaving the safety of a present job and traveling into uncharted waters. It may mean staying where we are and blooming where we are already planted. Either way, it's important to connect with the environment that brings out the best in each of us.

2. **Align Work with Passion**

   Every job has its share of mundane tasks. Those tasks don't have to put out the flame that burns inside of us. It is our own responsibility to fan into flame the gift God has placed inside us. We can't settle for the comfort zone and security of a job that we are not passionate about. Like Bill Pollard, we must take a leap of faith to pursue our passion.

3. **Trust that God Has Called You to Work for a Purpose**
   We all struggle to find the right balance between earning a living and serving a purpose. This tension is both normal and necessary because it helps shape our journey.

DISCUSSION GUIDE

Part 1: Individuals looking for meaning and purpose at work

1. What do you love doing? What are you most passionate about?
2. What is your greatest satisfaction at work?
3. Are you in an environment that fully utilizes your talents and skills?
4. What would you do if you knew you couldn't fail?
5. Create your ideal job.

Part 2: Organizations who want to discover the true purpose of their business

1. Other than making money, why do you exist? What purpose do you serve?
2. How does your organization add value and contribute to the community, customers, and employees?
3. How does your work environment help employees find meaning and purpose in their work?
4. How will fulfilling your organization's mission make your organization competitive and profitable?

Notes

1. C. William Pollard, *The Soul of the Firm* (Downers Grove, IL: The ServiceMaster Foundation, HarperBusiness, Zondervan Publishing, 1996), 19–20.
2. Ibid., 20–21.

3. Ibid., 14–15.
4. Ibid., 130.
5. Ibid., 46.
6. Ibid., 46–47.
7. Ibid., 57.
8. Ibid., 57.
9. Ibid., 58.
10. Ibid., 23.

2

Success

From success to significance

For I know the plans I have for you, declares the Lord, plans to prosper you and not harm you, plans to give you hope and a future.

—Jeremiah 29:11

Issue:

How do I define success?

The owner of the seventy-five-employee manufacturing company was ready to turn management of the family business over to his son. Three of us sat at a table in Mark's office, when suddenly, the dad slammed the business plan on the floor and lashed out at his son, Mark. "You're an idiot! I can't believe what a loser of a son I have! I didn't build this business to have you destroy it!" Mark sat quietly in his chair, expressionless. The owner walked out of the office, disgusted. I was stunned. I searched for something to say that would comfort Mark. After an awkward pause, Mark said, "It's nothing new. He's been like that his whole life."

I followed Mark's dad out of the room. I looked him in the eye and asked, "Do you love your son?" He paused for a moment and then answered, "Of course I love my son. It's just that I spent thirty-five years busting my butt to give him a better life. I don't want him to throw it all away." Then he added, "I worked hard to be a success, and I don't want to lose that."

Mark's father defined success by working long hours and making a lot of money. While he loved his son, his pursuit of success had cost him dearly. He had become a financial success and a personal failure: a seventy-year-old man with plenty of money but nothing to show for it. As a father, he left money, but no legacy. He left only pain and an emotionally abused son.

Solution:

Expand your definition from making money to making a difference.

When I was working with Mark and his father, I read a wonderful book, *Halftime: Changing Your Game Plan from Success to Significance*, by Bob Buford. The book provides tremendous insight into how we define success. Bob likens a business career to a football game. In the first half of our life, we pursue success. We work hard, sacrifice, and expend energy to become financially successful. In the second half, we focus on significance, giving our experience, time, talent, and energy toward making a difference in people's lives and leaving a legacy. Bob Buford's book crystallizes how important it is for us to take a hard look at how we define success.

The next two stories describe how two leaders came to redefine their success and lead lives of significance. Bob Buford, founder and chairman of the Board of Leadership Network, shows us how precious time is and that *now* is the time to live a life of significance. Jerry Colangelo, chairman of the Phoenix Suns Basketball Club and the former chairman and CEO of the Arizona Diamondbacks Baseball Club, provides an example of a business and community leader who has learned that success is fleeting but significance can last a lifetime.

BOB BUFORD
"From Success to Significance"

ob Buford understands the appeal of pursuing financial success. As the president of a successful cable television company, the Leadership Network, he loved the excitement of business. He was also successful in his personal life; he had loving relationships with his wife, Linda, and son, Ross. As Bob approached middle age, however, his thoughts started to focus on the next part of his life. He pondered a deep question as he entered the second half of his life: "What is most important in life?" Little did he know that the answer to that question was a phone call away.

Bob wrote his book from the lessons he learned during a very difficult time. One of the most powerful chapters, "Adios, Ross," tells about the tragic loss of Bob's one and only child, Ross.

On the evening of January 3, 1987, Bob got a call from his brother Jeff. Jeff, obviously upset, told Bob that Ross and two of his friends had tried to swim across the Rio Grande, a wide and unpredictable river that separates southern Texas from Mexico. His next words would change Bob's world forever.

"Ross is missing in the Rio Grande,"[1] Jeff said, his voice heavy from the weight of such news. Over the next long moments, Bob learned that twenty-four-year-old Ross had decided to join two other young men to try to capture the experience of what it was like for illegal aliens when they cross the dangerous watery border into the United States, the land of opportunity. Ross had no thought that this could be the last adventure of his earthly life.

Jeff told Bob that the third young man had survived and was frantic about finding his two friends. Bob arrived at the Texas–Mexico border, the Rio Grande Valley, before daybreak the next day to join the search, which was already well underway and coordinated by the Texas Rangers. Airplanes, helicopters, boats, trackers with dogs—Bob hired anyone and anything that could help the rescue effort. But several hours later, with no sign of either young man to give him hope, Bob faced the fact that he would never again see Ross in this life.

After all efforts had been exhausted, Bob returned home. The search continued, but it would be spring, four months later, before Ross's body was found, ten miles downriver. Earlier, during the cold winter months as Bob lived in an odd world between having and not having his son, the family found a handwritten copy of Ross's will on his desk at his Denver home. Dated February 20, 1986, it had been written less than a year before the fatal accident. But Ross's words warmed his father over that winter:

> Well, if you are reading my will, then, obviously, I'm dead. I wonder how I died? Probably suddenly, because otherwise I would have taken the time to rewrite this. Even if I am dead, I think one thing should be remembered, and that is that I had a great time along the way. More importantly, it should be noted that I am in a better place now.[2]

Ross's will ended with these words:

> In closing, I loved you all and thank you. You've made it a great life. Make sure you all go up instead of down, and I'll be waiting for you at heaven's gate. Just look for the guy in the old khakis, Stetson, and faded shirt, wearing a pair of Ray-Bans and a Jack Nicholson smile. I also thank God for giving me a chance to write this before I departed. Thanks. Adios, Ross.[3]

More than ever before, Bob realized how much he lived in two worlds. The first is the crazy business world of meetings, phone calls, deadlines, deals, profits, and losses. Bob explains, "That world is like a cloud; it's going to perish. The other world I live in is where Ross is now—the world of the eternal. And it's the reality of that latter world that allows me to respond, with confidence: Adios, Ross, *for now*."[4]

It is this eternal perspective that makes Bob passionate for life and deeply aware of the responsibility to make the most of each day. Bob especially likes George Bernard Shaw's quote, "I rejoice in life for its own sake. Life is no 'brief candle' to me. It is a sort of splendid torch which I've got hold of for the moment, and I want to make it burn as brightly as possible before handing it on to future generations."[5]

Ross lived each day of his life like that, with enthusiasm, passion, and joy, the one reason Bob considers his son a hero. Each day was fully used, not squandered in any way. Bob tells people, "[Ross] didn't shortchange himself, even though his days among us were so few. Ross's death, while tragic, was an inspiration to me to burn brightly while it is day."[6]

In spite of this tragedy, or perhaps because of it, Bob maintains a positive, passionate attitude. Most people are never the same after the tragic loss of a child. The incidence of subsequent divorce is high. Many people question the presence of God, and some reject God altogether. Few are able to deal with the loss in such a profound and significant way and to touch others deeply. But Bob has.

When I interviewed Bob, I wanted to talk with him about Ross, but I was apprehensive to ask such personally sensitive questions. I expected to meet a distinguished man with a reserved demeanor. I found a man full of passion.

Bob explained, "After Ross's death, my wife came to me and said, 'Let's sell the house,' which was her way of saying that material things meant less to her. It gave me the perspective that material things are not that important. For me, it gave me a sense of the whole of life, not just this part of life. There is a lot more to life than this brief period we are in. You either believe it or you don't, and I really, really believe it.

"There are two ways of processing events in life. One is reason and one is faith. Let's say our life is three feet long. Most of life is reasonable up to a point. We can use our reason for two feet and eleven inches. However, that last inch is incomprehensible. It makes no sense. We can't process bad things like the Holocaust, personal tragedy, or Ross's death. We go as far as reason will take us, but the spark of faith has to bridge the gap."

As I spoke to Bob, I couldn't help but contrast his life with that of Mark's dad. Bob had physically lost his son, yet Bob was alive relationally and spiritually. He was living his life to the fullest and making a significant impact on this earth. He was squeezing everything out of the life of the present and was excited about someday seeing Ross again in eternity. Mark's dad, on the other hand, had his son physically close to him, yet father and son tragically were living lives of relational emptiness.

I asked Bob what advice he would give Mark's dad—a man who is miserable because he is retired, is in good health, but doesn't know what to do with the rest of his life—and to Mark, a young man who has mentally decided to coast through the rest of his career.

Bob responded, "I believe God has planted spiritual DNA in every human being. He has a destiny laid out for each and every one of us. We can choose to accept that destiny or not." He also believes that it is absolutely critical that people don't ever let their brains coast. "Don't mentally retire on the job and put your plane on autopilot. Work will become increasingly sterile and meaningless. Everyone will know that you have done that. You will become more cautious and become increasingly worried that younger people are out-competing you. You become risk-averse. It's not good for you and not good for your organization."

Bob continued, "Secondly, don't physically retire. The idea of retiring to full-time leisure is a very dangerous idea. I have seen too many cases where people spend more time on toys and less time on relationships. I have seen too many people wind up in divorce."

Instead of taking such a passive role, Bob suggests people consider finding a parallel career, one that addresses two questions: What am I good at, or what have I achieved? What am I passionate about? The foundation of this advice is Bob's belief that God calls and equips everyone with talents to pursue his or her unique calling. It is up to each person to find a place to use those gifts and to fulfill a God-given destiny. This may not even involve much change. Bob suggests that we take our gifts and talents into account and fit them into what means the most to us: family, business, or volunteering, either part or full time. Says Bob, "The most important thing is to embark! Get going!"

Bob also believes in the Law of Unintended Consequences. He explains, "People discover in business that you embark with a plan, and even though things often turn out very differently than you planned, they do have a way of turning out. If you never embark, they will never turn out. For example, experts in the stock market will tell you that the market moves up big on twelve days a year, but the timing is utterly unpredictable. You have to be in the market in order to capitalize on the upturn. If you are on the sidelines waiting to time your move perfectly, it will never happen. People pursue their calling in the same way. They say, 'I will stay in my job now, and someday I will pursue my dreams.'"

Bob understands how difficult it is for people to pursue their dreams, but he believes strongly that it's sometimes as simple as taking a leap of faith. "I choose to believe that it is God who speaks quietly within us," Bob says, "that it is He who put the question deep within. And when we discover the answers, He reveals the meaning He has chosen for us to enjoy; He unveils the goal He has been keeping for us all along. I love how Paul puts it in Ephesians 2: 'For we are God's workmanship, created in Christ Jesus to do good works, which God prepared in advance for us to do.'"

"People are now living active lives into their eighties and beyond," Bob states. "People have a whole second adulthood that their grandparents never had. In many cases we have an extra twenty to thirty years of active adulthood remaining. What are we going to do with these extra twenty to thirty years? Many people don't need to work in order to live and survive. Most people spend a tremendous amount of time, energy, and resources toward their business but rarely do we apply the same time, energy, and resources toward the second half of our lives."

But Bob is a realist. He knows that, though few people want to put their careers ahead of their families, it happens. People want to be successful, and the pull is hard to resist. Choosing how we want to live is no less important for the second half of our lives than it is for the first. In fact, Bob tells people, "You have the freedom to decide whether you want the rest of your years to be the best of your years."[7]

Bob Buford leads a significant life encouraging thousands of people like Mark, you, and me to make a difference during this brief time we have on this earth. He understands the pursuit of success, and he understands the pursuit of significance. He invites each of us to ponder the question, "How can I make the rest of my life the best of my life?"

JERRY COLANGELO
"From Me to We"

Jerry Colangelo is a leader who has redefined the word *success*. In business terms he's the multimillionaire former owner of two successful sports franchises, the Phoenix Suns Basketball Club and the Arizona Diamondbacks Baseball Club. More important than success to Jerry, however, is leading a life of significance.

"Success, unfortunately, is measured by how well one has done financially," explains Jerry. "In my mind, success is having your priorities right and being able to make a difference in other people's lives. For me, my priorities are God, family, and making a difference in the community." Jerry's shift from success to significance has been a long journey. Along the way, he turned to God, which helped him shift the focus of success from *me* to *we*.

Jerry Colangelo had dreams of being a big success in sports. In high school, he was a star in both baseball and basketball. In 1957, his senior year, he made the Illinois All-State High School Basketball Team. He received sixty-six scholarship offers from all around the country and received six offers from major league baseball franchises. At the age of eighteen, Jerry had a bright future ahead of him. He chose to attend the University of Kansas because they had the best basketball player in the country, Wilt Chamberlain, and the best chance to win the NCAA Championship.

Life, however, didn't cooperate with Jerry's dreams. During his college years, things didn't go as he planned. Wilt Chamberlain left Kansas to play for the Harlem Globetrotters. His dreams of winning a NCAA Championship dashed, Jerry returned home to attend Illinois State. Unfortunately, NCAA rules kept him from playing basketball for a year. To support his family, he worked for the City of Chicago Heights in the sewage department. It was a humbling experience for a well-known athlete. Although an excellent basketball and baseball player throughout college, upon graduation, he was left with broken dreams. Due to injuries, he had to quit baseball, and in basketball, he was never chosen in the NBA draft. His career in sports was over.

With his dream of being a successful athlete now shattered, Jerry turned to the business world. He went into the tuxedo rental business with an old friend in Chicago Heights. For three years, Jerry poured everything into the business, working long hours and plowing whatever profits were made back into it, all to no avail. His business venture was a failure. At twenty-six years old, he found himself out of work with no future plans, struggling to support his wife, Joan, and their three young children.

Jerry was ready to redefine what success meant to him. He recalls, "Prior to this experience, it was all me, myself, and I. I considered myself pretty capable of taking care of things. Whatever life threw at me, I could handle. I was so busy doing my thing, trying to build my business, that I didn't have a good picture of where I really needed to be in my life."

Jerry's wife Joan had been attending a small Baptist church, and Jerry started going with her. Because of Joan, Jerry began to understand and depend on his faith in God. He found that when a person humbles himself before God, things change: priorities, attitudes, and relationships. "I finally realized that I couldn't do it myself," Jerry explains. "I didn't know where I was going to be the next day, because I had nowhere to go, no place to turn."

In his book, *How You Play the Game*, Jerry describes an extraordinary occurrence that took place. One day Jerry sat down at the kitchen table and, having nothing to do and nowhere to go, took his wallet from his pocket and started cleaning it out. As he was tossing away random scraps of paper, he found a business card, crumpled and worn. Jerry guessed he'd been carrying it around for about two years. He remembered his father-in-law handing it to him one day, mentioning that Jerry should meet this man.

Jerry had become busy with business and a growing family, so he forgot about the business card. As he looked down at the all-but-forgotten piece of paper, Jerry figured, "Why not?" He had lots of spare time and nothing to lose. In fact Jerry was at the bottom of his game—twenty-six years old, making only $50 a game playing in a semiprofessional basketball league at night. The next morning Jerry called the man, Dick Klein. Dick invited Jerry to come to his office for an informal chat. Jerry agreed.

As it turned out, Dick owned an incentive merchandising company that assisted companies in putting together gift packages and other programs to give to clients, distributors, and suppliers. He ran a one-person shop and was swamped with work. He hired Jerry to help in the business, but Jerry soon found that Dick's real passion was to start a National Basketball Association (NBA) franchise in Chicago. Jerry immersed himself in the incentive business and, at the same time, had the opportunity to be a part of Dick's dream of having a professional basketball team. Jerry soon found himself learning everything about the business side of sports from the ground up. As a result of calling Dick Klein, Jerry capitalized on the privilege and opportunity of birthing the Chicago Bulls, one of the most successful sports franchises in basketball.

During the Bulls' second year, the NBA expanded, adding franchises in Seattle and San Diego. The following year, the NBA expanded to Milwaukee and Phoenix. Jerry was in demand, and he was looking for an opportunity to become a general manager. He received an offer to become general manager for the new Phoenix basketball franchise for a salary of $22,500 per year. Jerry and his family moved to Phoenix in 1968.

Finally, Jerry's faith and business came together. "Joan and I had had an opportunity to chaperone a group of teenagers for a Christian youth organization called Young Life," says Jerry. "It made a big impression on me because it helped me see what was important to young people. When we moved to Phoenix a year and a half later, I mentioned this experience in the newspaper. Many families from the Young Life organization welcomed us to the Phoenix community. Being a part of the community meant a great deal to us."

Not only did Jerry recognize the importance of community from a personal viewpoint; he also recognized its value from a professional standpoint. The NBA was a relatively unknown commodity in Phoenix. He knew that success would start with a win-win relationship with the community. "From the start, my attitude was, 'This city doesn't owe us anything. The people of Phoenix do not owe us anything. We have to earn their support.'"[8]

From his start as general manager to his eventual ownership of the Phoenix Suns and Arizona Diamondbacks, Jerry worked toward building a positive relationship with the community. He credits his faith and his commitment to integrity as the cornerstones to building a long-term relationship with the community. Jerry recalled, "The greatest thing you can say about a person is that he has integrity. I started with nothing financially. I got a 'character loan' to get me up and running. A character loan is what you receive when you have no capital."

Jerry credits his faith as the single most important factor in his success. "Life isn't easy; it's a challenge," Jerry explains. "Successful people are those who can deal with challenges successfully. The truth is, the more public you are, the more opportunity you will have to fail, and fail in the most public and sometimes most embarrassing manner. You're dealing with the media, you're dealing with corporations, you're dealing with big business and high finance. In that potentially volatile mix, it's inevitable that you will make mistakes; a trade doesn't work out, a player doesn't live up to expectations, the arena needs more seats, the parking lot is too small, and so on."[9]

Jerry recalled one of the most painful experiences of his career. In 1986, a drug scandal hit the Phoenix Suns. Three players and two former players were arrested on drug charges. Although the charges never amounted to anything criminal and the case never went to trial, Jerry's reputation was dragged through the mud.

Phoenix was deluged by the media, and reporters were like hounds on the hunt. Jerry was the one they went after. They did their best to bring into question Jerry's character and reputation, and it looked as if all the work the organization had put into the community was going to go down the drain. Unable or unwilling to separate the man from the franchise, the media attacks made Jerry an object of ridicule. He was booed at games. It made no sense to him. Eventually, as is typical, the incident blew over and went away. But how did Jerry survive the storm? He explains, "Looking back, I couldn't see myself dealing with all of this without my faith."

Jerry Colangelo's thirty-two-year partnership with the Phoenix community is not a story about winning or financial success; it's a story about significance. "Over the years, I learned that things happen for a reason," says Jerry. "I once thought that success was being in the right place at the right time. I came to understand that it's God's plan, not mine. What pulls at my heart is to meet the needs of our community. God has given me a platform to bring together businesses, municipalities, social organizations, and charitable organizations to address all the needs of the community. My position gives me an opportunity to have more of an impact. I want to do as much as I can within reason to make as much impact as I can."

Ironically, evidence of Jerry's significance came from an old foe—the media. The *Arizona Republic* voted him Arizona's most influential sports figure of the century. The article read, "For changing the very scope of the community in which we live, Colangelo overwhelmingly was selected as Arizona's most influential sports figure of the century by the *Arizona Republic*'s sports staff. If this had been a horse race, Colangelo would have been Secretariat."[10]

CONCLUSION

How we define success is important in shaping our lives. Success is generally defined in terms of achievement, fame, recognition, material possessions, and wealth. In a word: *outcome*. Significance, on the other hand, while less tangible, concerns the *process*. Significance is importance, meaning, relevance, and value. Success drives us by a desire for tangible things; significance guides us by a desire for something greater than what is tangible.

Three common characteristics led Bob Buford and Jerry Colangelo on their paths to significance.

1. **A Sense of Urgency.** Because this life is short, the preciousness of life continually challenges Bob and Jerry to prioritize what is most important. They live lives of daily significance, doing what they feel is most important every day. This sense of urgency translates into a passion for the moment. You can sense their liveliness.

    Psalm 39:5 reminds us, "Each man's life is but a breath." If we are looking to lead lives of significance, we need to make it a priority *today*. It's not too late, regardless of our age. Bob Buford offers the challenge: "The most important thing is to pull the trigger. Embark! Get going!"

2. **A Sense of the Whole of Life.** Both leaders have a sense of the whole of life, rather than just the part of life we can see today. Bob Buford commented that Ross's death gave him a sense of the whole of life, providing him with an eternal perspective that helped him transcend the pain of his immediate tragic loss. He could have focused on the pain, but he chose to live the remainder of his life being significant in the present, while maintaining the hope of seeing his son again in the future. Jerry Colangelo learned to put wins and losses in their proper perspective. As a

result, no obstacle or loss could prevent him from helping his community.

When we feel stuck or slowed down by pain, obstacles, or circumstances, we can remember that God has a bigger plan than what we are seeing in front of us. When we take a step back and sense the bigger picture and the whole of life, we can see our situation from a different perspective.

3. **A Sense of Significance.** Bob and Jerry are driven by their calling and sense of significance, not their ego. They believe they are here to make a difference in other people's lives. Everything they do is for something more than just a tangible result. Bob has a passion to unleash the potential energy lying dormant in churches today. Jerry's passion is to help meet needs in all aspects of the Phoenix community. They each have a hunger to leave a legacy that affects thousands of others.

While we may not all be asked to change the world, we can each affect one person in a meaningful way. What if Mark's dad had focused on building a relationship with him? What kind of impact would that have had? Others need us. We can make a big difference in their lives right now. And that alone makes our lives significant.

DISCUSSION GUIDE

1. How do you define success?
2. How do you define significance?
3. If you had only one more year to live, what would you do with your year?
4. What are the obstacles that keep you from doing what you are passionate about?

5. If you were to make a shift from success to significance, what would it look like?

6. What legacy do you want to leave others?

7. What small thing can you do today that would make a difference in another's life?

Notes

1. Robert P. Buford, *Halftime* (Grand Rapids, MI: Zondervan Publishing, 1994), 55.
2. Ibid., 55–57.
3. Ibid., 57.
4. Ibid., 59.
5. Ibid., 59.
6. Ibid., 59.
7. Ibid., 166.
8. Jerry Colangelo with Len Sherman, *How You Play the Game* (New York: American Management Association, 1999), 61.
9. Ibid., 62.
10. "Colangelo pushed Valley teams' buttons," *Arizona Republic*, (December 26, 1999): Section C, Pages 1 and 8.

3

Courage

From choosing the easier wrong decision to making the tougher right decision

Be strong and courageous. Do not be terrified; do not be discouraged, for the Lord your God will be with you wherever you go.

—Joshua 1:9

Issue:

How do I do the right thing when I'm pressured to do otherwise?

Shutting my office door behind him, my boss said, "I think Mike has a nose problem. I heard that he's heavy into cocaine. I want you to get some dirt on the guy and fire him."

I was taken aback. Mike had been an excellent employee and one of my best salespeople for years. My first reaction was to do the right thing: I wanted to talk honestly to Mike. If, in fact, he did have a problem, I wanted to help him get his personal and professional life in order. But when I mentioned this approach to my boss, he blew up, saying, "I don't care how you do it, just get rid of him. I want him out of here now!"

I was caught between a rock and a hard place: I could do what was right and risk being fired myself, or I could choose not to make waves and be the "team player" as my boss would call it, and do the dirty work my boss had demanded I do. Well, I copped out and made the easier decision, the wrong one. I saved my job by unjustly taking the job of another. My boss's ego and my fear of unemployment hurt the entire staff. Not only did we lose a good employee; we also lost the trust of our sales team. The decision may have saved my job, but I lost a little piece of my soul.

Solution:

Walk with God in courage.

A time will come when a leader's faith will be tested beyond his or her perceived limit, a time when business pressure, intellectual logic, and fear gang up, to the point where an easier wrong decision takes precedence over a tougher right decision. Fear and discouragement keep us from doing the right thing. Conversely, courage enables us to rise above difficulty to reach new heights as a leader. This is the time when leaders need to be strong and courageous and do what's right.

In this chapter, you'll read the stories of the honorable Al Quie, former governor and congressman of the state of Minnesota, and Marilyn Carlson Nelson, former chairman and CEO and now member of the board of directors of Carlson, an 175,000 employee international hospitality company whose brands include Radisson Hotels, Country Inns & Suites, T.G.I. Friday's restaurants, and Carlson Wagonlit Travel. Although very different in position and circumstance, they learned that having the courage to do the right thing was life-changing, not just for them, but for a greater good that at the time could only be seen by God.

AL QUIE
"Having the Courage to Walk Away"

The State of Minnesota was in serious financial difficulty. The tension and bitterness between the Republicans and Democrats were at an all-time high as they tried in vain to balance the budget. The battle raged on for months as the recession of 1981 carried over into January 1982. Everyone was worn out, especially the leader, Republican governor, Al Quie.

Not only was Governor Quie tired of the battle with the Democrats; he was tired of dealing with the press. In reality, he knew he was avoiding the press because he was hiding something deep within him and wasn't ready or willing to confront it. "Every time a reporter asked me if I was going to run for reelection, I would say 'yes,'" the governor recalls. "Each time I said 'yes,' I would feel a sharp pain in my heart. I recognized that happens when I'm not totally honest with myself."

Governor Quie remembers being particularly concerned about a meeting he was to have on Friday with Betty, an outstanding reporter for the *Star & Tribune*. He knew that she was good at going after the truth, and the governor wasn't ready to see her because he wasn't ready to talk about his plans for reelection. "Even though I was telling people 'yes,' I wasn't at peace with that decision," says Governor Quie. "I was torn, and it was really affecting my mental health. Indecision has a debilitating effect on you. If you do what you don't believe, it will corrupt your soul. People in politics know what I'm talking about. If enough people do it long enough, it will corrupt the whole institution."

As his appointment with Betty drew closer, Governor Quie felt increasingly uncomfortable. But as Friday morning approached, he received the best news he'd heard in a long time. The National Weather Service had posted a winter storm warning due to a severe blizzard that had developed in the northern plains and was bearing down on Minneapolis. Governor Quie made one swift and decisive move: He called Betty to postpone the interview until the following week.

He and his wife, Gretchen, quickly drove to their family farm nestled in the countryside near Marine on St. Croix, Minnesota. Governor Quie explained, "The most satisfying feeling in a person is to be totally honest. In politics, many times you can't tell people right away; you need to sort things out first. I absolutely did *not* want to see Betty. I knew this blizzard would give me an opportunity to get away from the bombarding of my world and be alone in the presence of God."

Retreating to the family farm brought back some of Governor Quie's cherished memories. "I love blizzards," he says. In fact, one of his clearest memories is of a time when he was walking in the woods by the farm. Howling winds and blinding snow nearly swallowed him as he walked. But deep into the woods, it became quiet and still. He recalls, "I remember looking up and seeing the blizzard raging through the treetops, but the trees protected me from the wind. I experienced total peace and quiet. The snow fell gently down as the blizzard raged fiercely above. It was awesome! It was like being in the hands of God with the world raging around you." That memory had kept him grounded in some turbulent times, and it was giving him courage in this one.

As Governor Quie settled into a weekend of being quiet and listening to God, he played out the pros and cons of running for reelection. He quickly came to the realization that there actually was no dilemma. The solution had been there all along, but he hadn't really accepted it. Governor Quie knew in his heart that he wasn't going to run for reelection. He admits, "I hadn't had the courage to do the right thing. Fear and ego got in the way."

Still, he wasn't sure how to tell people that he wasn't running again. He was no quitter, but stepping out of office could make him look like one. Governor Quie explains, "When you say 'I'm not going to run anymore,' people will say, 'He couldn't take it, he's out of here!' When a person trains himself to be macho, be strong, be a man, face dangers, not show weakness, be in control, how do you let go of that?"

When the time came, the governor found two scriptures that helped him clarify his decision. In John 6:28–29, the people asked Jesus, "What must we do to do the works God requires?" Jesus answered, "The work of God is this: to believe in the one he has sent." In Mark 10:45, Governor Quie also saw how Jesus came "not to be served, but to serve."

Dwelling on those scriptures, the governor recognized that his ego and busyness were getting in the way of him being in tune to God. He realized that if he ran for reelection, he would be serving his ego rather than serving the greater good. "I was raised with the idea of helping other people," explained Governor Quie. He determined that he could do more good for the people of Minnesota if he didn't run for reelection. Partisan politics often keeps sides from working together, and the governor had a glimmer of hope that by forgoing another term in office, he could work with the Democratic leader of the state to help the people of Minnesota. "What I did know was as long as I was running, there was no way they would work with me," he recalls. "To the Democrats, I was the enemy; they would prove they won by making sure I lost."

By the end of the weekend, Governor Quie was comfortable with his decision and had mustered up the courage to do the right thing. It was time to announce that he was not running for reelection. He looked around him. The Twin Cities were beautiful after the big snowstorm. The sky was a deep blue, the air was fresh and crisp, and the entire city had a fresh blanket of pure white. There was an unmistakable newness and freshness about it. And that's exactly how he felt on Monday, January 26, 1982, as he announced that he would not seek reelection for governor of Minnesota.

"I was free!" he says. "From the moment I made my decision, my judgment was never again colored by my concern for reelection."

There was another benefit—one Governor Quie never dreamed about. After his decision, people saw him in a different light. His credibility improved because people sensed that he had sacrificed his career for a greater good, for their good. As the former governor explains, "You can't say it, think it, plot it, or plan it. People see the true spirit of service when it comes from your heart."

Shifting focus to the higher good broke the logjam of a bitter political battle. Governor Quie's courage to let go of power and ego allowed others to do the same. The budget battle stalemate, which had brewed for months, was resolved in three days.

Simply put, the leaders had to find acceptable ways to both cut spending and raise taxes. The Republicans were adamantly against raising taxes, and the Democrats didn't want to cut spending. Governor Quie called each leader from the House and Senate and met with them personally. He explained that he wanted to arrange a private meeting with the key leaders from both parties to resolve the budget. Then he asked them to pick all the necessary decision makers so the hard decisions could be made at the meeting.

Many leaders were hesitant because of the private nature of the meeting. Meetings were usually open to the press. Governor Quie clarifies, "I explained to them that if we brought in the press, the focus would be on looking good in the public eye, rather than having the courage to do what's best and right for the public." This time they met without the press.

With new conviction, Governor Quie helped each leader find the courage to focus on the higher good. Understanding the political risks he was asking each leader to take, he offered himself as a buffer. He told them, "If you feel a decision is too dangerous politically, you can blame me."

The meeting started Monday morning. By Wednesday night, both houses of the legislature had passed the bill to resolve the budget shortfall.

It's easy to be bombarded with the noise of our circumstances. Not only are we pressured by others, but the voice of our own ego deafens our ability to hear God's whisper. It takes courage to listen to God with a totally honest heart. It takes even greater courage to follow through on what we hear. In Governor Quie's case, he learned that it wasn't about choosing a right or wrong decision; it was about having the courage to see and follow through on the decision that had been whispering in his heart all along.

MARILYN CARLSON NELSON
"Having the Courage to Overcome Tragedy"

Marilyn Nelson had the life many people strive for. The eldest daughter of Curt Carlson, founder and chairman of Carlson Companies, Marilyn had wealth, influence, strong faith, a good marriage, a loving family, and an active professional and community life. Everything appeared to be going well until October 3, 1985. Her busy day at Carlson Companies was interrupted by the call every parent dreads: Her beloved nineteen-year-old daughter, Juliet, had been killed in an automobile accident.

Marilyn's world immediately spun out of control. "Even though I had a powerful faith, it was devastating," Marilyn explained. It is hard to imagine a tougher challenge than facing the loss of a loved one. As many people experience in the grieving process, at first, Marilyn was angry at God. Then she denied that God even existed, struggling painfully with how a good God can let something like this happen.

But after all the wrestling about Juliet's death, Marilyn tried desperately to make sense of the situation. She read the Bible and many other books and listened to different philosophers. But when all the voices on the pages and platforms were silent, she still had no answers—just more questions.

Marilyn tells people, "I knew I could choose to give up and put the pillow over my head, or I could fight back. I knew my options of becoming 'bitter or better' and wanted to learn from this experience. I never gave up. I continued to search, ask, and knock, and eventually the door got opened again. Slowly but surely, I gained insights that helped me heal and get better."

She explains that one of those moments came from reading the story in the Bible about the talents. In this story, a master goes away and asks his servants to invest their talents. While most of us see this as a metaphor for using our God-given talents, Marilyn found, through Juliet's death, that this was also a parable about time. "The only time we have is today," says Marilyn. "We should live each day as our signature day. We may have ten thousand days remaining, or it could be our last. If this day stood for all of time, is this a day you would want to have your name on?"

Out of the ruins of despair, Marilyn rebuilt her life, one moment at a time, one decision at a time, one day at a time. She tells others that leadership is about making decisions every day. She knows well that leaders are regularly faced with making compromises and that it becomes easy to rationalize those compromises. To Marilyn, true leadership is found not only in making the big decisions, but also (and perhaps even more so) in the little decisions that must be made every day. Those decisions prove one's greatness.

As painful as Juliet's death was, it helped Marilyn grow. "It gave me perspective," she says. "Once you lose something unspeakable, a loss you think you can't endure, and you survive it, other problems change in their perspective. For me, time and relationships are really precious."

Marilyn has grown stronger from adversity. It was a slow process of living a moment and a day at a time. She likes to remind people that none of us knows what is waiting in the next chapter of life. Every single day is important. We learn to take responsibility, yet stay open to seeing, hearing, and sensing God's direction.

After her daughter's death, Marilyn began to see little messages of hope coming her way. More and more, she sensed God at work in her life. One day her sister came to see her and, instead of having a good visit, they got into a painful conflict. Marilyn's sister, though trying to be supportive, told Marilyn to get on with her life. All of the emotions Marilyn had been carrying inside welled up and poured out. "I let her have it," recalls Marilyn. "I yelled and screamed at her and ran into my bedroom. I got into bed and fell asleep." Several hours later Marilyn woke up and went into the living room. Her sister was still there, sitting on the couch. When Marilyn asked her why she was still there, her sister calmly answered, "I was just waiting here until you woke up." That was a powerful, hope-filled moment as Marilyn deeply felt her sister's love toward her. Marilyn strongly sensed, "God is at work here."

Since then, Marilyn's strength has grown one day at a time in spite of continued trials and setbacks. In 1999, Marilyn's father, Curt Carlson, passed away. His death, like her daughter's, did not ultimately overcome her. Instead, it strengthened her to lead Carlson Companies into the new century.

Curt Carlson came from a background where money was scarce. His family lived in Sweden during the potato famine. Curt's father, Marilyn's grandfather, came to the United States, and Curt grew up learning that making money was very important. His life was about accumulating enough financial capital to be successful.

But Marilyn, never burdened with such a fear of scarcity, was passionate about people: attracting and nurturing *human* capital. During her leadership of Carlson, she wanted to empower people to do more together than they could do alone. This grew from her belief that God is at the core of relationships. By allowing God a place at work, people can be encouraged to find and utilize their talents. They begin to believe they can make a difference. Leaders need to create the environment that allows this to happen.

I asked Marilyn what she would want as her epitaph. She quoted Isaiah 40:29–31: "He gives strength to the weary and increases power to the weak. Even youths grow tired and weary, and young men stumble and fall; but those who hope in the Lord will renew their strength. They will soar on wings like eagles; they will run and not grow weary, they will walk and not be faint."

What is her advice for people who are struggling in pain or experiencing burnout? "You are not alone, God is with you," she offers. "There are little messages of hope that are out there. If you let them in, they will rekindle your hope and spirit." Marilyn herself is a message of hope to those who know her.

CONCLUSION

Courage is easily misunderstood. For many, courage is defined by doing bold or brave things. The underlying reason for the action may be ego gratification, power, or recognition. Demonstrating moral courage, on the other hand, is very much a private matter between you and God. Sometimes, as with Governor Quie, we come to a point where we know God is calling us to change our life's direction, and we must quiet our ego in order to hear God's whisper. Sometimes, like Marilyn Carlson Nelson, we are confronted with a painful blow that shakes the very foundations of our beliefs and we need the courage to renew and deepen our faith in God.

Whatever your situation, you (like these leaders) will probably be brought to a special place of tested faith and courage, a place where you will be challenged to go against the grain of common sense to move into the uncharted waters of illogical faith. Challenges, rewards, and blessings occur for all of us who make the choice to do the right thing.

1. **Common Challenges.** Governor Quie and Marilyn Carlson Nelson struggled intensely before finding the courage to move on with a new life. Whether the consequences they pictured were real or imagined, they faced fear and discouragement. In Governor Quie's case, he feared ending his political career and being labeled as a quitter. In

Marilyn's situation, her loss was devastating and her discouragement was enormous. Although public figures, they each had to take a private journey to reexamine their faith in God.

Both consciously came to a point where they exchanged their personal desires for a higher purpose and a greater good. Governor Quie put the citizens of Minnesota ahead of his career while Marilyn turned her energy to serving her employees and community. Having come to a point where their trust in God transcended their present circumstances, they took a leap of faith.

2. **Common Rewards and Blessings.** These case studies provide an excellent reminder that power and authority have little to do with money and position and everything to do with character and aligning your actions with your principles. Governor Quie accomplished more in his final year as governor and beyond because his actions expressed his desire to serve the greater good of the state. Marilyn's influence and authority is now based on her renewed faith and courage to overcome personal tragedy, rather than the leadership inherited from a famous father. Their personal decisions have benefited countless people.

Most of our lives are shaped by the decisions we make every day. It doesn't matter whether the decision we're faced with is big or small. What's important is to understand that every decision helps shape our character and destiny. We are either becoming who we want to be or who God wants us to be. Business demands, coupled with personal fears and ego, make choosing the wrong decision tempting. For that reason alone, it is even more important to take time to make sure our decisions align with our faith, values, and principles. It's wise to prayerfully consider God's counsel in all of our decisions. Asking ourselves these two questions will help guide us when choices must be made:

- What is the right thing to do?
- Am I willing to trust God's promise that He is with me in this decision, regardless of the consequences?

Deciding what is right and acting on our convictions can be a daunting task. We are different people in many different situations. We may never understand why God has placed a certain decision before us. Nevertheless, the one thing we have in common is that God has promised that He is with us *always*.

DISCUSSION GUIDE

Part 1: Individuals facing a difficult decision

1. What is the most difficult decision you are facing?
2. What are your fears and concerns regarding this dilemma?
3. What do you believe God is saying to you about this decision?
4. In your opinion, what do you think is the easier wrong decision?
5. What are the consequences and implications of making the easier decision?
6. What do you think is the right thing to do?
7. What are the consequences and implications of making the right decision?

Part 2: Individuals facing a difficult situation

1. How do you cope with your present situation?
2. What attitudes do you presently battle with?

3. How can you develop the patience to wait for God's answers?
4. What gives you comfort during this difficult period?
5. What messages of hope can you see?
6. How can you move forward with courage to transcend this difficulty?

4

Patience

From sprinting under pressure to running with purpose

Let us run with perseverance the race marked out for us.

—Hebrews 12:1

Issue:

How do I avoid becoming a slave to urgent, short-term pressure?

The corporate office was breathing down our necks. We had only forty-five days to achieve our fourth-quarter goal, or else. Our sales team had spent months developing a meaningful strategic plan. In that plan, our long-term goal was to build a base of loyal, long-term customers. We thought we were in the clear to work our plan, but that went out the window with a business shortfall in the third quarter. The downturn created the same old battle cry: Stop what you're doing! Create a short-term plan for business now!

We paid less attention to our existing customers so we could focus on getting immediate new business. The good news is we won the short-term battle. We achieved our fourth-quarter goal. The bad news is we lost the war. In the process of "doing whatever it takes" to achieve our short-term objective, we completely lost sight of our long-term goal—our overall strategic plan.

We asked our customers to accommodate our needs, and in the process ignored their needs. We were so busy getting new customers that we left our existing customers feeling unwanted, unappreciated, and used. While we fervently sought new business in the short term, two of our biggest and most loyal customers quietly let their contracts expire and went to a competitor.

Solution:

Develop patience to run a long-distance race in a 100 yard–dash world.

Patience and bottom-line pressure are like oil and water. They don't mix. Having the patience to work a long-term plan sounds great in theory, but in reality, short-term pressure often forces us to play another game. Pressure comes from both external and internal forces. The bottom-line expectation to produce, coupled with our internal pressure to succeed, takes us out of our game plan. We exhaust our energies sprinting from quarter to quarter, running a race dictated by pressure. With patience, we learn to run the race we have been called to run, in spite of the pressure that surrounds us.

In this chapter we will meet two leaders with a common trait, patience. Tony Dungy, head coach of the Tampa Bay Buccaneers football team from 1996 to 2001, transcended the outside pressure to produce. Archie Dunham, former chairman and CEO of Conoco Inc., an oil industry leader, and now independent non-executive chairman of Chesapeake Energy, transcended his internal pressure to succeed. Both leaders discovered that patience is the key to long-term success.

TONY DUNGY
"Pressure from the Outside: Sticking to God's Plan Produces Results"

The Tampa Bay Buccaneers walked dejectedly back to the locker room. The pressure was growing after another heartbreaking loss. Their 1996 NFL season was now an awful 0–5! The pressure to win grew stronger with each loss. Patience was growing thin. The players were discouraged and frustrated. The fans were tired of losing and wanted to see a winner. The media fanned the flames of discontent, claiming "same old Bucs—same old losers." The owners were remaining supportive but were quietly nervous. They wanted financial support committed to the building of a new stadium; losing the first five games was not going to help build a stadium. There was pressure to make a change . . . any change. Advice began to roll in from all sides. Change the quarterback! Run more! Pass more! Change the defense! Change the coaching staff! The pressure was mounting from all sides, and it pointed straight to one person: the new head coach, Tony Dungy.

To say that Tony Dungy felt pressure to produce would be an understatement. It took him fifteen years to become a head coach in the NFL. He was only the fourth black head coach in NFL history. Upon finally receiving his big opportunity, he was immediately surrounded by impatient Tampa Bay players, fans, owners, and community. "When are you going to win?" "How will you win?" "What changes are you going to make to win?"

Turning to Tony, what did all these desperate eyes see? Panic? Anger? Desperation? No. They saw a calm, patient leader who was keenly aware of his circumstances, yet was unwilling to allow short-term defeat to get in the way of his long-term plan for success. Tony recalls, "I was disappointed, but not discouraged. I prayed, 'Lord, you brought us here for a reason. You have something in store for us.' I felt our situation would make our story even better." Tony believed that God had a greater plan—one that transcended winning and losing.

To gain insight into Tony's patience and perseverance, it's important to understand a little more about his journey. When Tony was twenty-one years old, he was a rookie with the Pittsburgh Steelers, a young man who dreamed of becoming a successful player in the National Football League. He had been a star quarterback at the University of Minnesota, where he had twice been named most valuable player. Football was his top priority.

"Everything was going well," recalls Tony, "when I suddenly became sick with mononucleosis and was unable to play. The illness lingered for six weeks. I grew frustrated and impatient, not being able to do anything other than just wait."

Tony voiced his frustrations to his roommate, Donnie Shell. Donnie's response cut right to the heart of the matter. He turned to the impatient young man and said, "Football is the most important thing in your life, and God wants to see if that is above Him or below Him. Until you are ready to put football below Him, you will always be frustrated with your problems." Donnie's comments made Tony take a look at himself and his priorities.

From that point on, Tony placed his football career in God's hands. His favorite Bible verse, Proverbs 16:3, demonstrates that the key to Tony's patience lies where he places his faith. "Commit to the Lord whatever you do and your plans will succeed." Tony's career and success have been built not only on seeking God's will and timing, but also in patiently working God's long-term plan in a business with short-term goals.

After his playing career ended, Tony moved into coaching. He patiently waited for the opportunity to become an NFL head coach. Though a highly successful defensive coordinator/assistant coach with the Minnesota Vikings, he was continuously overlooked as a potential head coach. In 1993 the Vikings had the number-one defense, seven head coach jobs were vacant, and Tony wasn't offered even one of the opportunities.

NFL owners, on the whole, desire a coach with one thing on his mind—winning. As a prospective coach, Tony didn't have that mindset. While interviewing with owners, he openly shared his values. "While winning is important, it should be a result of doing what's right," he told them. He wanted to win, too, but believed in a long-term goal, one that transcended winning and losing. His goal was to develop his players to become not only the best they were capable of becoming, but also to be good community citizens and role models for today's youth. Tony's beliefs and values may have cost him job opportunities, but he was at peace. He recalls, "I was comfortable waiting for the right opportunity. I had faith that the Lord would place me where I was supposed to be."

Tony received his big break in 1996 when he became the head coach of the Tampa Bay Bucs. "I believe I'm in Tampa because it's God's plan," says Tony. Clearly, he didn't set out to get the job, and he didn't move heaven and earth to get there. In fact, the owners were looking for a high-profile coach, and Tony didn't fit that description. Jimmy Johnson was the first choice, but he turned down the offer to go to Miami. University of Florida head coach Steve Spurier was the second choice; however, he chose to stay at the university. Knowing he wasn't a top choice, Tony's attitude remained peaceful: "If it's the Lord's will, I will get the job, and, if not, life goes on," he told himself.

When he interviewed for the Bucs' head coach position, he was completely honest. "I never sacrificed my integrity," says Tony. "I shared everything, including my view on winning, my faith, my leadership style, and my desire for the Bucs to become role models and good community citizens. We openly discussed the expectations we had of each other. I have a responsibility to respond to their authority, yet in the things under my authority, I have to do what I believe is right. They respected what I stood for and gave me full support."

Tony was excited about the owner's willingness to support his long-term plan, but he also knew he had his work cut out for him. The Bucs had built one main reputation since their first season in 1976: They were losers. They carried a bad reputation on and off the field. Tony inherited a team with a track record of losing, poor attitudes, and maintaining low expectations.

One of the first things Tony did was to build a coaching staff of men who shared his values of character, personal accountability, and teamwork. The coaches and senior players were given the role of helping younger players become all they were capable of becoming, both on and off the field. From the beginning, Tony set up a system for the older players to help the younger players. He told them, "It's your responsibility to counsel the younger guys." Tony was certain that leadership by example, accountability, and unselfish teamwork would lead to long-term success for the Bucs and for the players themselves.

Tony explains that at the first meeting on the first day of training camp, they talked about the high standards of their game plan and the high expectations of each individual on the team. He defined success as "doing the very best you are capable of doing." Of course, it's good when that translates into wins, playoffs, and a Superbowl, but no such outcome is guaranteed. "If all we think about are Superbowls and winning," says Tony, "then we will compromise and take our focus off being the best we can be. I talked to every player on the team. I asked each one to be a part of the solution. Help us set a new direction. I told them, 'The guys that handle responsibility will be successful. The more we accept personal responsibility and help each other, the quicker we will achieve our success. Now, let's all be accountable to each other.'"

Tony's long-term plan was challenged when the team stumbled to a disastrous 0–5 start. But the new coach's steady perseverance was reassuring. He didn't point fingers or place blame. Instead, he told them that he wasn't looking to make quick changes but was going to solve the problems. After each loss, they reviewed the things they did wrong and made the necessary adjustments for improvement. "The losing streak was difficult, but I saw how the players were growing," Tony recalls.

Tony modeled everything he stood for. In the midst of adversity, he modeled the character and patience he wanted in his players. He had been on a losing team. As a young player on the San Francisco 49ers, Tony watched head coach Bill Walsh. They lost their first seven games, but three years later, the team was in the Superbowl. Tony knew it was crucial for him to be a model of patience and consistency in the midst of defeat.

As coach, he knew his patience had made an impact when Dave Moore, a tight end, came to him after the first season. Dave told him, "The whole team, including me, was waiting to see you just lose it. Nobody can go through this and be the same. We were all waiting for you to go off on us." He never did.

Today, the Tampa Bay Bucs represent a different kind of success story. In the NFL, success is still defined by winning. With just a few years under Tony's leadership, the Tampa Bay Bucs became winners, the 1999 NFL Central Division champions. But this is a success story that transcends winning football games, and the Bucs are much more than an NFL title.

Dungy was let go from the Buccaneers in 2001 and became head coach of the Indianapolis Colts, where he remained until his retirement in 2008. But elements of his legacy remained in Tampa Bay. Under the leadership of Coach Jon Gruden, the Bucs went to the 2002 Superbowl and won it against the Oakland Raiders—an amazing journey for a team that had been dubbed losers.

Tony Dungy believes that even when success is delayed, patience is ultimately rewarded, even in a business that is so demanding. "When you have success, it is easy to stick with your convictions," explains Tony. "But when success is delayed, to stick with what you believe is right is difficult. I believe patience is rewarded. God works in ways that appear to be illogical. You have to be willing to stick with God's plan even when you don't understand it."

When people in the business of football are asked to describe Tony Dungy, they use words like *patience*, *commitment*, and *consistency*. Tony Dungy became one of the most loved and respected coaches in the NFL.

ARCHIE DUNHAM

"Pressure from the Inside: Trusting in God's Plan Prepares You for Success"

Archie Dunham was bright, ambitious, and frustrated. A middle manager for Conoco Inc., he felt he had plateaued at age thirty-six. "I was impatient," he says of that time. "Things were not moving fast enough for me." Though doing well at Conoco, his impatience made him restless and unhappy.

While living in Houston, Archie became an active member of Spring Baptist Church. The church was growing rapidly and needed land to expand. The pastor asked Archie if he would chair a committee to negotiate with seven physicians who jointly owned the land south of the church. Archie agreed to chair the committee and, in his typical management style, selected the highest-powered and brightest business executives, lawyers, and developers to be on it. Then there was the final committee member, a deacon named Luther, a man of God who was twice the age of any other member.

Archie felt the assignment would be quick and easy. He thought, "Piece of cake. With the level of talent and skill this committee possesses, the deal will be negotiated in no time." In reality, negotiations broke down quickly. After each negotiation session, with little progress made, the committee would regroup and revise its strategy. Following each meeting, Luther politely asked Archie the same question, "Archie, are you seeking God's help with this problem or are you trying to solve it yourself?" Each time, Archie replied, "Of course I'm seeking God's direction." Inwardly, he knew he wasn't. Six weeks later, Archie finally allowed God control of the situation. To his amazement, the problem was quickly resolved, and the physicians agreed to sell the land.

Later that year, relaxing on the swing in his backyard, he realized that he had turned his salvation over to God but never turned over control of his life and career. The revelation of his lack of trust humbled him. There on that swing, Archie prayed, "Lord, if you want me to live in hot, humid Houston for the next thirty years, if you want me to stay in this job for the next thirty years, I will do it if that's the plan you have for me." That brief moment on the swing changed Archie's destiny, because finally Archie completely gave up control of his career. From that moment came a meteoric rise from frustrated middle manager to chairman of the board and CEO of Conoco Inc. He listened for God's will and he had the faith to trust in God's plan.

Six months after he accepted the idea of living in hot and humid Houston, if that was God's desire for him, Archie was transferred to cool and beautiful Newport Beach, California, as executive vice president for a Conoco subsidiary, a job he never imagined having. Archie and his family loved their new environment. He enjoyed his new responsibility, and his family enjoyed living in San Clemente.

Two years later, Archie received a call from the president of Conoco. The president told him that Conoco's headquarters was going to move from downtown Houston to the suburbs. More importantly, he wanted Archie to be the project manager. Remembering the lesson he learned on his swing, Archie told the president he needed to think about it. After much prayer, Archie felt that God was telling him to remain in California. He called and respectfully declined. He recalls, "Fifteen seconds after turning down the offer, I began to get calls from my former bosses who were now vice presidents of the corporation. They exclaimed, 'Have you lost your mind?' and 'This is a great opportunity! We called the president and said that you were a bit hasty and needed another week to think about the offer.'" Archie agreed and decided to pray for guidance again. This time, he was even more convinced to stay in California and turn down the job opportunity in Houston. Six months later, Archie was named president of the Conoco subsidiary.

Over the years, Archie remained steadfast in his commitment to follow God's career path for him. It wasn't always easy. He still struggled with his impatience from time to time. Archie recalled a time when he once again grew frustrated and impatient to move up the corporate ladder. About that time, he received a call from a prestigious board search committee inquiring to see if he was interested in becoming the CEO of one of the largest Fortune 100 companies in the country. "It was everything I dreamed about," Archie says. "It offered a great challenge, a nice city to live in, and a fantastic compensation package." He was excited to pursue the job, but didn't have total clarity about the move. He valued his long tenure with Conoco, yet was intrigued by this enticing offer. Once again, he prayed. Finally, he said, "Lord, I am going to leave Conoco unless you stop me." Eight hours later, he received a call from the chairman of the search committee. They had placed the search on hold. Archie felt wonderful! He knew this was a tremendous confirmation to stay at Conoco.

Six weeks later, he received a call at 5:00 A.M. from the chairman of DuPont, Conoco's parent company at the time. The chairman quickly stated, "Wake up and brush your teeth! I'll call you back in ten minutes to discuss something important with you." Ten minutes later, Archie was named president and CEO of Conoco Inc.

On May 11, 1998, the *Wall Street Journal* announced that Conoco Inc., and its parent company, DuPont, were going to separate, making it the largest initial public offering in U.S. corporate history. That announcement set in motion a series of events that created the most stressful time in Archie Dunham's life.

The initial public offering of Conoco totaled $4.4 billion. The resulting dilemma weighed heavily on him. "We had a fiduciary responsibility to entertain offers from third parties to acquire all of the company," explains Archie. "As a member of the DuPont board, my role was to evaluate all offers, but in my heart, I wanted Conoco to be a separate company because I knew it would be best for Conoco's employees. It was extremely stressful. We knew that we could choose to accept an offer from a 'super major' oil company and find ourselves no longer part of DuPont but part of another company instead. That would mean Conoco being broken into pieces, with thousands of employees being laid off and management being terminated." This was the ultimate test of faith for Archie. As he humorously recalls, "Before that, I had blond hair; now it's gray."

Once again Archie found himself in the kind of situation in which he first turned his career over to God. He and his wife tried to get away from the stress. On August 30, 1998, Archie and his wife went to Colorado for a four-day vacation, but they had no rest. The fax machine kept printing out new offers. Walking into the backyard, he found himself in a familiar setting. Sitting on the swing, he struggled between his will and God's will. His greatest concern was for the thousands of Conoco employees, yet he knew he had to honor his fiduciary responsibility to evaluate third party offers to the best of his ability. It boiled down to Archie's will for Conoco versus God's will for Conoco. "I had to totally trust that His outcome would be the best for me, my management team, and our employees," Archie recalls. "I came to the deep understanding that God's will was the perfect solution for me, for the company, and for Conoco's employees. Finally, I was ready to accept His outcome for our company. I was at peace."

The Conoco initial public offering was the largest and most successful in the history of the New York Stock Exchange. In the end, everyone won. Employees kept their jobs and enjoyed the stability provided by Archie's leadership.

While Archie's story may say, "Turn your career over to God and you'll be successful," there is another, more significant message.

Following God's plan is the ultimate win-win solution. Of course, we don't use God for our success; He uses our talents for His purposes. God often chooses to work through those people He can depend on. Those who are faithful with a little are given more. But we also enjoy the benefits of following His plan. In the process of fulfilling God's will, we grow stronger in character and more capable in tough situations. He tests us through challenging circumstances to see if we have the character and capability to follow Him. While difficult for us, this is an extremely important time in which God is shaping us into unity with His purpose. It is no coincidence that this powerful combination of character and capability grooms us for success in the business world.

In Archie's case, God was preparing him to handle the Conoco initial public offering. The raises and promotions were byproducts of following God's plan. It took twenty-five years of testing and refining to prepare Archie for the important role he played in Conoco's sale and future.

Archie Dunham is a leader with more than thirty-five years of training in patience. He was forced to think through the moral, ethical, and financial implications of an important decision that affected thousands of lives. Archie Dunham is where he is because he has followed God's plan and has provided value to others. In the same way, when we have the patience and courage to follow God's perfect plan in obedience, we too become more valuable to others.

Archie is no longer impatient. Now he is passionate about sharing his message of trusting God's perfect plan. He tells people how important it is to trust the Lord in all their major decisions and to be patient. While God doesn't promise that someone will be financially successful, He does promise to provide His best outcome. Says Archie, "Some choose at thirty to follow His plan; some people wait until they are sixty years old; some never do it. I think those who go their own way miss out on what God's perfect plan is for their life." Archie was willing to trust God, and, as a result, he is happier and healthier than his plans would ever have led him to be.

CONCLUSION

Tony Dungy and Archie Dunham demonstrate the patience to run a different type of race, one in which they allow God's timing to set the pace. They demonstrate their ability to persevere in running the race God has marked out for them. They were steadfast and consistent in working with a purpose in spite of difficulties and pressure. These men relied on three traits to help them succeed through patience and perseverance.

1. **Prayer.** These men used prayer as a means to overcome impatience. In Tony's situation, it gave him the strength to hold on to his plan in spite of outside pressure. In Archie's case, it helped him let go of his impatience to climb the corporate ladder. Prayer was the most practical tool these leaders used for making tough decisions. As leaders, they were bombarded with advice from all sides. Their consistent communication with God kept them focused on their main purpose, rather than distracted by the immediate obstacles in their path.

2. **Perspective.** I'll always remember the insightful words of my friend Andy Anderson. He said, "Larry, your problem is that you have blinders on. You're so focused on the bottom line, you can't see the world around you." He was absolutely right. I associated our sales team with a greyhound dog race. We all ran as fast as we could to catch the rabbit. Nothing came into our sights except our goal. We

sprinted from goal to goal but had no sense of purpose. In reality, we were just running in circles.

Goal achievement is extremely important, but it's easy to lose perspective. Our sales team expended all its energy trying to feed the insatiable quarterly revenue god, promotion god, and personal security god, and it was never enough. Over time, we eventually became slaves to short-term goals, living our lives from quarter to quarter.

Tony Dungy and Archie Dunham had perspective. They saw a bigger picture in the midst of their circumstances, and this helped them work within their purpose. Perspective gave them a context from which to make sound decisions. Perspective helped them see a higher purpose in their work—one that transcended their immediate problems. Tony saw his losing streak as an opportunity to build character in his players. Archie learned how to wait on God, rather than jump at the first promotion that came his way. Perspective helped these leaders set the pace of their race rather than letting their circumstances set the pace.

3. **Preparation.** Tony and Archie relied on patience and perseverance as necessary instruments for growth. In essence, patience was preparing them for greater service to God. The long-distance runner works toward success by gaining endurance. Endurance helps the long-distance runner grow stronger by increasing his or her capacity to run, often by weathering pain. In the same way, the more Tony and Archie practiced running with perseverance instead of caving under pressure, the better prepared they became for the next circumstance, the next challenge, and the next opportunity.

We live in an impatient world. The business world has trained us to run the 100-yard dash, where success is measured in terms of tangible results such as speed to market, sales, profit/loss, and market share. While these goals are necessary and important, the challenge is in following God's plan when the business world demands we react quickly to another plan. Often, God's plan seems to make no sense in a business environment because we try to measure it using the same tangible measurements we use to determine our business success. Ultimately, winning the marathon instead of the 100-yard dash comes down to two questions: What kind of race do we want to run? Who is setting the pace?

As Rousseau stated, "Patience is bitter, but its fruit is sweet." Many of us struggle with patience because it's so hard to see any immediate benefit. God's perfect plan for our life may not involve tangible evidence today. Often, it's the things we can't see in the present that prepare us for a significant future. But we can run boldly and with perseverance the race that God has specially marked out for each of us.

DISCUSSION GUIDE

1. What is the greatest external pressure you face?
2. What is the greatest internal pressure you feel?
3. Describe the ideal pace of your professional life. Your personal life?
4. What prevents you from working at the pace you desire?
5. What can you do to run the race God has marked out for you?

5

Leadership by Example

From what you do to who you are

Let your light shine before men, that they may see your good deeds and praise your Father in heaven.

—Matthew 5:16

Issue:

How do I demonstrate my faith in a politically correct and diverse work environment?

I was walking home from school with my friend, Freddie, who was also Jewish, when two tough-looking teenage boys came up to us. One of them turned to Freddie and said, "Hey, kid, are you Jewish?" Freddie, looking down, quietly said, "No." Then the stranger turned to me and asked the same question. "Hey, kid, are you Jewish?" I looked up and innocently answered, "Yes." To my shock, the teenager spit in my face. I couldn't figure out why he would single me out and spit in my face. It didn't take long to convince myself it's not a good idea to reveal your religious beliefs. It's best to keep them to yourself.

Many years later, I developed a personal relationship with Jesus Christ. Even so, I still didn't want to share my faith with others. I hadn't liked being labeled as a Jew, and I didn't want to be labeled as a born-again Christian. I had carried that lesson through my childhood and the beginning of my business career. Being quiet about one's faith in the workplace made perfect sense. Why would I reveal my faith and risk my career?

Solution:

Let who you are speak for what you believe.

Sharing one's faith at work is a highly sensitive issue. Revealing your inner faith invites stereotyping, defensiveness, and debates about political correctness, not to mention the legal implications.

On the other hand, we don't want to hide the very essence of who we are. There is nothing wrong with revealing the source of our values, decisions, and priorities. In fact, integrating our faith and work paves the way to a more meaningful and productive work environment. This chapter is not about whether we are allowed to bring our religion to work. This is not a debate on whether God should be at our workplace. God *is* in our workplace! God doesn't wait for us at the end of the day to see how our day was in the secular world. He is with us wherever we go. Integrating work and faith is about bringing who we are to work.

To help us gain perspective on this very personal dilemma, we'll hear the stories of two leaders who have struggled with this issue. Jeff Coors, former president of Coors Brewing Company, and John Beckett, former president of R.W. Beckett Corporation, a manufacturer of residential oil furnaces, and author of *Loving Monday: Succeeding in Business Without Selling Your Soul*, have found that integrating work and faith is a challenging, meaningful, and rewarding experience.

JEFFREY H. COORS
"Moving from Doing for God to Being with God"

More than thirty years ago, Jeff Coors was a young, aggressive junior executive well on his way to taking over his father's and uncle's roles as leaders of Coors Brewing Company. Although his career was on the right track, he was struggling in his spiritual life. He had been a church attendee his whole life, but it wasn't until August 1974 that Jeff developed a deep personal relationship with God.

"It was the first time in my life that I had a clear understanding of how biblical principles applied to my life. My immediate desire was to apply these principles at work," Jeff explains. Jeff quickly realized he was caught between two worlds: It was okay to discuss biblical principles with church members on Sunday, but it was taboo to discuss them at work Monday through Friday. Jeff recalls, "I felt very lonely. My pastor had no experience to give advice in this area, and my fellow Christians felt that work and faith should be separate."

As he continued to grow in his understanding of the power behind biblical principles, Jeff continued to wrestle with how best to reconcile his spiritual self with his business self. Being open about his faith was both risky and frightening, considering he came from a public family that ran a public company.

To compound his split-identity issues, Jeff, like many so many executives, was a doer. He was an action-oriented and goal-driven self-starter. While Jeff loved God and wanted to do His will in business, Jeff's will and determination got in the way. "I was just so zealous doing things for God," Jeff says. But he found that when he tried to do the work of the Lord, he tended to get ahead of God rather than being led by Him. Jeff used the force of his own will to get things done. For example, zealous to be a peacemaker, Jeff interpreted that to mean making others be peaceful—bumping heads and forcing the peace.

Jeff struggled to find the right way to integrate his faith and work until 1989, when things came to a head. He felt he had reached a position of power and status to do great things for God, but he was not at peace. Now the president of Coors Brewing Company, he was a powerful local, state, and national leader. And he was incredibly over-committed.

Before he realized it, Jeff found himself over-involved and way over-extended. As president of Coors, he was managing the beer business, ceramics business, and several other businesses owned by the company. Jeff was on a dozen boards, leading a business project in Denver called Blueprint for Colorado, and starting a Christian prep school. "I felt as a good follower of Christ, God had raised me up to do all these things," explains Jeff. "It was way too much." All the doing took a toll. Jeff admits that he overlooked his responsibilities to his wife and family.

He realized it was time to do some soul-searching, so he took a sabbatical. Jeff's turning point came when he attended Crossroads Discipleship Training, a program for people who, like him, were in midlife and trying to sort things out. During the program, the work/faith equation became much more integrated.

Jeff attended the program believing his time in the workplace was over, that God was calling him out of business and into a ministry. Unfortunately, he had been led to believe by several people (including pastors) that business was "of the world" and that as he matured in his faith, Jeff would eventually be led to a higher calling, outside of business. Jeff recalls, "In many ways it left me with a feeling of guilt that as a businessman, I was a second-class Christian."

But Jeff kept searching. After much prayer and discussion with wise people, he discovered that his business was a calling and that it was his. Jeff Coors was right where God wanted him to be. Says Jeff, "That moment radically changed me. It confirmed to me that business was a legitimate calling equal to any so-called 'ministry.'"

Jeff has found how to integrate his faith and work. He explains, "I am much more into being *with* God than doing *for* God. He has given me a real peace about being in the business world, and I have a better understanding of my role. It boils down to being the kind of person God created me to be. I use the Lord's Prayer as my guide: 'Thy will be done on earth as it is in heaven.' I believe God has a desire to have His will done on earth. Being the person He created me to be will bring Him glory and fulfill His original plan."

Now, instead of changing the world for God, Jeff simply honors his relationship with God and others around him. He understands that God calls us into a relationship first with Him and secondly with the people He has placed around us. Jeff, now president and CEO of Golden Technologies Company, Inc. and director of Graphic Packaging Holding Company, used to be president and CEO of Graphics Packaging International Corporation. That company's values statement reflected Jeff's wisdom:

Respect for People

We value each person's intrinsic worth and uniqueness. We acknowledge everyone's contribution and honor his/her opinions. Our work environment is open, honest, supportive, and fulfilling. Our company is built on trust.

Responsibility for Actions and Results

We keep promises. Each person is empowered to make the organization succeed and is 100 percent accountable for his/her actions. We challenge the status quo, promote continuous improvement, and reward excellence. We lead by example and do not avoid difficult decisions. We invest in our people and operations for future growth and profit. We work safely, comply with laws, and are a good neighbor. We meet our commitments to shareholders, customers, and employees today and tomorrow.

Relationships with Each Other

Our success is built on quality relationships. We communicate openly and truthfully in a timely manner. We encourage constructive feedback. We are committed to each other and have fun together. We are helpful and compassionate. We treat others the way we want to be treated.

Jeff tells people, "It all boils down to respect and relationships with people. Respecting people is part of who I am. I hold people in ultimate respect, thank them for their contributions, and congratulate them for their successes. Sometimes it is simply being there for them when things don't go well." The values statement has resonated throughout the company. Jeff explains that they started by casually talking about it. Now it's a key foundation of the business.

Today, Jeff states he's still a work in progress. He focuses on trying to listen and be a part of God's plan instead of getting out in front of Him. He admits, "I have to fight that all the time. There are still times when I feel that I'm not being bold enough. I'm not by nature a bold person. During those times of struggle, I make it a point to really stay close to God. However, I can tell you that everything is so much better than before." Through his journey, Jeff has found that he has more peace by working with God than by working for Him.

JOHN D. BECKETT
"Demonstrating Your Faith by Living Your Faith"

John Beckett's newfound relationship with God had created a new life, but it had also created a new dilemma. "How should I relate my faith to my work? Can these two worlds that seem so separate ever merge?" he wondered. For years, John thought that it was most appropriate to follow the rules created by modern culture: Believe in God on Sunday, and get to work on Monday.

John was thrust into the leadership of the family's manufacturing business, R.W. Beckett Corporation, following his father's sudden death. Shortly after, fire nearly consumed the corporation, yet with tremendous effort, the business survived and even began growing rapidly at a rate of 20 percent per year.

Along with work, which was nearly all-consuming, John and his wife, Wendy, were thoroughly devoted to raising their four children (later to become six). They were growing in their faith and seeing the effect it had on their relationship with family and friends. Yet, John found ever-increasing questions about how to blend his newfound faith with his work.

In John's book, *Loving Monday: Succeeding in Business Without Selling Your Soul*, he describes a defining moment in which he came to the decision that integrating faith and work was the key to running a successful business. He begins by explaining that he had been raised to understand that companies and their employees were better off working in a union-free environment. As a realist, John knew that business leaders could only do so much to influence that decision in their workplace. Under the law, workers are free to form or affiliate with a labor union. But when John thought about a union coming in at R.W. Beckett, he was terrified.

As often happens, the thing he most feared came to pass. John recalls, "When I received the news that an organization attempt was underway, that fear became almost paralyzing in its intensity. Then the fear turned to anger—anger that some of our employees would consider such a course, rather than talk with our management about their concerns."[1]

John decided to enlist the help of a local labor attorney, a man who was known for his tough approach to organization attempts. He agreed to help, but before he had a chance to get very involved, he died of a sudden heart attack. Under increasing pressure, John prayed a heartfelt prayer. "Faced with our attorney's death, I almost concluded we should handle the situation by ourselves," says John. "That was until I happened to be reading from the book of Proverbs, and to my surprise, my eyes fell upon a very pointed verse. In the translation I was reading at the time, Proverbs 12:15 said, 'Don't act without the advice of counsel.' Well, within a few days we had located an attorney from Cleveland who, as it turned out, gave us outstanding advice, helping us guide our month-long campaign to rebuild our employees' confidence in our company."[2]

More than anything, John feared that such a change (unionizing) would destroy leadership's direct relationship with Beckett's then-thirty employees. It seemed clear to John that an outside organization, whose purpose is to stand between employer and employee, could never have the same care and concern for the workers that R.W. Beckett had had over the years. Instead, it most likely would put a wedge where there had been a close working relationship. John's leadership was solidly based on the biblical model of Ephesians 6 that said employers should conduct themselves with their employees in the same caring and compassionate way that God treats people.

John writes, "So with conviction, good counsel, and a sound strategy, we shared our views and concerns with our employees, all within the tight guidelines imposed by the National Labor Relations Board. A vote was taken, and the overwhelming decision of employees was to stay union-free."[3]

John believes that God helped guide them through that difficult time. But he views it as a big wake-up call, too. "I realized that we had neglected communication," recalls John. "Many aspects of our employee policies and practices were not well understood. Some of our benefits were substandard, and we promptly took steps to improve them."[4]

Such a potential shake-up made John realize that he could not continue living in two separate worlds. It was time to integrate his Sunday beliefs with his Monday through Saturday workweek.

John answered three questions related to incorporating faith and work:

1. How did the R.W. Beckett Corporation successfully integrate faith and work?
2. How was the concept of sharing faith appropriately communicated within a diverse work environment?
3. What have been the consequences of integrating faith and work?

The answers to these questions, summarized from John's book, *Loving Monday*, are outlined as follows.

How did the R.W. Beckett Corporation successfully integrate faith and work?

John's wake-up call made him realize a vital key to the kind of leadership he sought: You can't leave your heart at the door when you come to work. If anything, he realized that compassion and respect are at the very core of a successful business. John backed up his compassion with action, as demonstrated by his following three commitments.

Develop the compassionate enterprise; blend accountability and compassion for successful results.

The first truth John realized was that compassion and accountability complement each other. In business, we try to separate the two, and, inevitably, an imbalance occurs, particularly away from compassion and toward accountability. As John sees it, "Compassion without accountability produces sentimentalism. Accountability without compassion is harsh and heartless. Compassion teamed up with accountability is a powerful force—one which we have found can provide a great incentive to excel."[5]

John provides several examples of how the combination of compassion and accountability benefit the R.W. Beckett Corporation:

- When a person is passed over for a promotion, management will follow up, show appreciation to the employee for stepping forward, and then point out how he or she can strengthen his/her qualifications. Management will then encourage the person to apply for advancement in the future.
- When a customer has had a reversal and needs an extension of credit, the company is mindful of the risk but is also understanding, going the extra mile to be of help when it is wise to do so.

- When an employee is going to be terminated, the company provides the employee with as much dignity and compassion as possible. John explains, "First, we go through whatever process is necessary to make a firm decision. This is an analytical step, dealing squarely with reality. The second is the termination itself, which should be carried out with all the compassion we can muster. An effort should be made to cushion the transition, such as a severance arrangement and possibly the use of outplacement services. But the key is to see the process as redemptive, a step which God can use to accomplish His larger purposes in the person's life and in the organization."[6]

Be committed to employee growth and development; create blueprints for success.

At the core of John's compassion for others lies a passion and belief that every employee has an ability to successfully fulfill his or her God-given destiny. "I feel we are at our highest and best as an employer if we can provide a context for growth and enable our employees to find and fit in with God's blueprint for their lives."[7]

Encourage employees to be committed to their families and to prioritize family over work.

John recognizes that the work/family balance issue is one of the most critical issues facing businesses today. He knows that the choices between work and family can be difficult to make, especially as the demands of work grow due to downsizing, which places heavier burdens on those who survive the cuts.

Recognizing the difficulty of this dilemma, John made a major commitment to prioritize family over work. "Our priorities should be ordered like this: First, our relationship with God; then commitment to family; and then commitment to our work and vocations."[8] The R.W. Beckett Corporation backed up these beliefs with these family-oriented policies:

- **Maternity Leave:** The company gives the employee an opportunity to stay at home for up to twenty-six weeks. During this period, the employee maintains his or her income at one-quarter the normal level. The company will loan the employee an additional one quarter, providing up to half of his or her normal wages. For up to three years after the birth of a child, the employee has the option of returning to work part-time, sharing his or her job with another employee, or doing work at home. (The latter two options depend on availability.)
- **Adoption:** The company provides a $1,000 adoption benefit and, in certain cases, has provided paid time off where travel to a foreign destination is necessary to complete the adoption.
- **Travel Policies:** The company tries to limit the nights employees must be away from home. R.W. Beckett does not insist, as some do, that employees travel over Saturdays to take advantage of reduced fares.
- **Open Houses and Company Visits:** Management recognizes that most young children have no idea what jobs their parents do during the day. They simply see Mom or Dad disappearing and reappearing on a daily basis. The company has open houses and company visits in which children are invited to visit on a special day so parents can show the children where, how, and with whom they work.
- **Company Newsletters:** The company provides family-oriented newsletters, mailed to employees' homes, with human interest stories to help build bridges between work and family.

- **Hiring Family and Relatives:** The company recognizes the risks of hiring relatives but also sees the rewards. The company maintains safeguards, such as not allowing family members to report to each other, and overall has found the policy beneficial to both families and the organization.

How was the concept of sharing faith appropriately communicated within a diverse work environment?

These written statements are communicated to all stakeholders of the R.W. Beckett Corporation:

Vision
Our vision is to build a family of companies, each of which serves its customers in distinctive and important ways, and each of which reflects the practical application of biblical values throughout.

Guiding Principles

- **Focus:** We are a Christ-centered company.
- **People:** We build and maintain solid relationships of respect among ourselves, our customers, and our suppliers, encouraging the growth and well-being of each employee.
- **Conduct:** We will conduct ourselves with dignity, adhering to the highest ethical and moral standards.
- **Work environment:** We aspire to be a great place to work: a progressive, dynamic, and continuously improving company that embraces world-class practices in quality, timing, involvement, and simplicity.
- **Stewardship:** Our business is a trust, and we will be good stewards of every resource in our care.

- **Citizenship:** We want to serve others, helping meet human needs in the community and beyond.

John justifies the forthright reference to being a Christ-centered, biblically based company, something that happened quite naturally because of the company's basic values. No one imposed these values; they evolved from the process of the company defining itself. When a company's values and the bottom line clash, priorities get reevaluated. John explains, "As we point out in explaining our vision to employees, every enterprise is guided by *some* point of view, some undergirding philosophy. Our management has elected to have biblical tenets and principles serve as that guide."[9]

Of course, employees don't have to agree. John continues, "We are careful to be inclusive of any employee's faith, making sure religious beliefs have no bearing on his or her opportunity to work with or advance in our companies; rather we seek to view all with equal appreciation and respect."[10]

What have been the consequences of integrating faith and work?

It has now been more than thirty-five years since the union situation changed John's view about integrating faith into his work. The consequences of integrating the two have been twofold: financial and interpersonal.

Financially, the R.W. Beckett Corporation has grown from a small, unknown company with $4 million in revenue to a nationally known company that, with its affiliates, has revenues of approximately $100 million. In terms of market share, the company has grown from a company with minimal marketplace recognition to commanding 75 percent of the North American market.

John is excited when he talks about the impact incorporating faith and work has on people. "I can honestly say that I have never been challenged on any level, from employees, management, our board, our customers, or our suppliers regarding this issue," he says. "We are constantly surveying our employees, vendors, and customers for their feedback. The response has been consistent. They view us as people of integrity. We are people who are consistent and can be counted on."

John has learned that incorporating faith and work does not force one person's will over another's. In fact, it provides the opposite; it provides freedom for individuals to fulfill their destiny in the workplace.

John's message to others is one of true appreciation. "In America, we are very privileged to have the freedom to integrate our faith and our work," says John. "I find each day is important and filled with opportunity—not just to 'survive the rat race,' but to actually have a part, however small, in consciously knitting what I do into God's larger purposes. If I can do that in a way that serves the Lord and brings glory to Him, as well as blessing our employees and business associates, I will have considered my work to be of great value."[11]

CONCLUSION

Integrating work and faith is about bringing who we are to work. Each of us is completely free to be a godly leader at work. No one can separate us from our faith. Still, we wonder, "Who am I at work?" "Do my actions, behaviors, decisions, and speech reflect God's nature?" Many of us feel we have to work for God like we work for our boss. We need to do something, achieve something, change something. Maybe, as Jeff Coors learned, we are called to simply be with Him.

Jeff Coors, John Beckett, and other successful leaders follow three principles when integrating their faith and work:

1. **Leadership by Example.** In Matthew 5:16, Jesus said we were to be salt and light. In essence, we are to reflect God's nature for others to see. We reflect God's nature in our business decisions, our relationships with our employees and customers, and our behaviors. There is no easy or pre-formulated process to successfully integrating faith and work. It's an everyday process of walking with God. We are constantly bombarded with decisions: Should I remain quiet if there is an opportunity to speak up? Should I listen instead of speak? Should I share with someone in need?

   Ralph Waldo Emerson said, "Who you are speaks so loudly I can hardly hear what you are saying." Simply put, we can relax, focus on our relationship with God, and allow His presence to shine through us.

2. **Respect.** A common principle followed by Jeff Coors, John Beckett, and other leaders I interviewed was respect for others. These leaders have a strong belief that every individual should be treated with respect and dignity. Respect honors diversity and others' rights. Respect for others comes from the heart. It isn't a program we must follow; it's part of our nature as godly leaders.

   The simplest guide is to follow the golden rule, Matthew 7:12, "Do to others what you would have them do to you." I know of a large Minnesota-based multinational company whose business is primarily based in Southeast Asia. The differences in culture and religion resulted in difficulties agreeing on major business issues. This company found that using the golden rule helped establish a foundation of mutual respect that led to open communication and meaningful working relationships.

3. **Compassion.** John Beckett showed us that love plays an important role in business. At the R.W. Beckett Company, showing compassion for employees, customers, and vendors is part of their business. When it comes to bringing our faith to work, no organization and no person can stop us from loving others and showing compassion for a fellow worker. No one can prevent us from praying for another person. No one can prevent us from being who we are except ourselves. In 1 Corinthians 13 we are reminded that "love is patient, kind, is not self-seeking, does not envy, does not easily anger and always trusts, always hopes, and always perseveres." Our workplaces are desperately looking for people to express that kind of love. We can do that every single day without ever asking permission or forming a special interest committee to look into the matter and develop a plan.

We've seen the challenges and opportunities of integrating faith and work. We come from unique backgrounds and have diverse viewpoints. We work in vastly different situations, but we all can integrate our faith and work. First and foremost, we must have the courage to be who we are as godly people. Nothing speaks louder. As for a specific dilemma we may have at work, we can prayerfully bring the issue to God and others. Questions like the ones that follow will help clarify the situation and bring us ideas for how to proceed.

DISCUSSION GUIDE

1. Do you feel free to demonstrate your faith at work? Describe your comfort level as it relates to being who you are (mentally and spiritually) at work.

2. What keeps you from expressing your faith at work?

3. Specifically describe the boundaries you feel are appropriate as they relate to integrating your faith and work.

4. What do you feel is God's will for you in the integration of your faith and work?

5. What specific action steps will you take to find more peace and fulfillment in the integration of your faith with your work?

Notes

1. John D. Beckett, *Loving Monday: Succeeding in Business Without Selling Your Soul* (Downers Grove, IL: InterVarsity Press, 1998), 55. Used with permission.
2. Ibid., 56.
3. Ibid., 57.
4. Ibid., 57.
5. Ibid., 110.
6. Ibid., 111–112.
7. Ibid., 95.
8. Ibid., 130.
9. Ibid., 146.
10. Ibid., 146.
11. Ibid., 170.

6

Yielding Control

From "surrender means defeat" to "surrender means victory"

For whoever wants to save his life will lose it, but whoever loses his life for me will find it. What good will it be for a man if he gains the whole world, yet forfeits his soul?

—Matthew 16:25

Issue:

How do I deal with circumstances that are beyond my control?

I facilitated a strategic planning session for a small, rapidly growing health-care organization that was experiencing significant marketplace change. The changes were fast and powerful, and had to be dealt with swiftly or the company would go under. In a meeting, we identified all the changes and came up with good strategies to address them. The executive team was apprehensive, but overall they were unified about the changes the organization had to make.

But not Jan, the vice president of operations. She resisted every single new strategy and had an argument for every change that needed to take place. In essence, she was the biggest control freak on the team. The greater the uncertainty, the greater her resistance. Unfortunately, Jan became a major stumbling block in the strategic planning process. The true tragedy was that Jan was extremely talented and capable, yet she was quickly becoming a liability to the organization. She desperately tried to control the circumstances surrounding her as the riptide of change swept her away. The executive team had to respond quickly to the changes that were occurring, and cooperation from Jan's position was critical to their success. As a result, they had to replace Jan.

Jan's situation brings up a challenging question. When is it time to take charge and when is it time to relinquish control?

Solution:

Do my part, and let God do His.

Every day, many business leaders try to control situations that they have no control over. The harder they flex their muscles, the more they lose control. Generally, the greater a leader's power, the harder it is for him or her to relinquish control to a higher authority. Many leaders call on God like they call on a consultant, to help them with their problems. They may go as far as delegating some control, but in no way will they relinquish total control.

In this chapter, we will learn about two leaders who were faced with turbulent conditions. Tad Piper, former chairman and CEO of Piper Jaffray Companies, an investment management firm, tells his story of surrendering control and power. Jim Secord, one-time president and CEO of Lakewood Publications and former publisher of *Training* magazine and various books and newsletters, shares his story about cooperating with circumstances. In both, we learn that surrendering control to God is a better plan than trying to take charge of things beyond our control.

TAD PIPER
"Relinquishing Control"

Tad Piper, former chairman and CEO of Piper Jaffray Companies, typified the high-powered executive. He was a take-charge person who made things happen. Tad was the third-generation Piper to lead the highly respected investment firm with a 100-year tradition of excellence, service, and integrity. He enjoyed all the trappings that came with the position: wealth, community standing, and power. Executives like Tad have a powerful need to be in control of the circumstances that surround them. Tad believed that with his power and influence, nothing was beyond his control, until one day in April 1994, the bleakest day in his life.

That was the day the most respected financial newspaper in the world, the *Wall Street Journal*, proclaimed Piper Jaffray bankrupt. The *Journal* reported that Piper Jaffray's fixed income portfolio manager had used borrowed money to amplify returns and had invested in derivatives—hybrid investments developed to boost yields at a time when bond prices were soaring and yields were crashing—which exposed investors to a higher degree of risk than expected. After six interest rate increases in ten months, the bond and derivative markets crashed. Investors in Piper Jaffray's bond fund, many of whom had enjoyed spectacular returns, saw the market value of these funds drop over half a billion dollars.

The effects were felt around the world. Pension funds declared disastrous results on their balance sheets. Individual investors were furious. The *Wall Street Journal* claimed Piper Jaffray's liabilities exceeded their assets and that they didn't have the means to reimburse their customers for the losses. Tad attempted to respond to the article and put the truth in context, but it was too late. Reporters, lawyers, and government regulators burst through the doors of the Piper Jaffray institution with the intensity of a raging firestorm. Tad quickly found himself in unfamiliar territory. He was in the world spotlight, and he had experienced a blow that brought him to his knees.

"I felt terrible," Tad recalls. "Here we had a 100-year-old company whose mission was to serve our clients and not disappoint them, and I felt we had let them down. I also felt betrayed by the people I trusted. I just couldn't believe this was happening. I repeated over and over, 'What did I ever do to deserve this? Why me?'"

The enormous personal burden Tad felt became all-consuming. He explains, "I had to figure this thing out because the potential consequence of not sorting it out was staggering. My reaction was 'Well, so be it. I'll roll up my sleeves and dig us out of this mess. I'll get the press straightened out, I'll fight the lawyers, I'll visit every unhappy customer, I'll fly to every branch office to explain the situation and console every angry employee, and I'll fix the market.'"

As valiant as Tad's efforts were, no matter what he did, he couldn't quell the firestorm. Relentless pressure came from every angle. Day after day, Tad dealt with the problem and its consequences: class-action suits, a vicious press, unhappy clients, and government regulators. The same questions pounded him: "Were you at fault?" "Did you make false promises?" "Did you falsely advertise?" "Are you going out of business?" The pressure grew worse with each passing day, and underneath the surface, Tad was crumbling.

After four months in a focused "I can fix it" mode, Tad had neared the end of his rope. A sense of desperation crept in. There was no light at the end of this tunnel, only darkness. His earlier thoughts ran through his mind. "I just gotta get this right. There's too much riding on this to screw it up! I must handle it! I'm not a quitter!" In the middle of this battle, Tad saw only problems. He was no longer fighting the lawyers and the media; the battle was in his own mind, and he was losing.

Then one day Tad received a gift from an employee who himself had gone through a painful situation. The small package contained a tape recording of a sermon along with a note that read: "Heard this, it helped me, maybe it can help you. God bless." Tad appreciated the gift from a caring friend and slipped the tape in his briefcase.

Two weeks later, Tad remembered the tape and popped it into his cassette player. The sermon, on the story of Job, got his attention because he could relate to Job. Intellectually, Tad knew that God was and is the center of the universe; Tad wasn't. He had learned that lesson two years earlier when he had admitted he was an alcoholic. Although rereading the Alcoholics Anonymous *Big Book* and the Book of Job helped Tad cope temporarily, he was still not at peace. He simply could not relax until he fixed this thing. Too much was at stake.

A few weeks later, Tad reached his breaking point. It wasn't any one particular incident; it was sheer exhaustion that did him in. Completely overwhelmed, he couldn't go on. "I remember lying awake in my bed, yet another sleepless night, in total despair, thinking, 'Oh my God! I just can't handle it anymore. It's just not possible. I can't do it. It's not possible. It's just too much!' At some point I remember praying, 'Lord, I just can't do it, so you have to!' All of a sudden, I remembered, 'Wait a minute, I'm not alone. I don't have to do it alone. There is help.'" Relief flooded through the broken man. He had finally reached the place where he knew God was in control and he himself was not. Tad's crisis was over. The crisis wasn't just about the circumstance he was in; it was also about his need to surrender to God.

Life was different after that night. Tad was at peace, and it showed. Slowly, his world began to change. "Because I knew God was with me all the time, I was able to navigate through some pretty troubled waters while keeping myself on an even keel. I worked just as hard, but it was much easier with my Partner (with the big P) with me. I was calmer. I became more rational about what I was capable of doing. I allowed others around me to do their jobs. The calm that was in me allowed others to be calm."

His relationships improved overall, but Tad's relationship with his lawyers improved most. Although they were on the same side, Tad had been in constant conflict with them. The lawyers were looking out for the company's best interests, and Tad was looking out for the clients' best interests. Those differing viewpoints created stress. When Tad relaxed, he started to see a bigger picture solution. His calmer demeanor allowed for better communication to develop between him and his lawyers. They eventually started to work together in harmony.

In addition to being more at peace, Tad opened up. Before, Tad felt he had to be strong for others. He could not and would not show his vulnerability to others because that would be a sign of weakness. Tad realized that his surrender to God wasn't defeat, but was victory over the circumstances he had tried to control. Not being in control was actually liberating! It was no longer about hiding his weakness, but about sharing in God's strength.

Tad discovered that communicating his true vulnerable self was much more of a blessing to others than trying to be strong for them. Tad recalled the time he and his wife Cindy openly shared their pain to all the spouses at the Piper Jaffray national managers' meeting. Tad explains, "The ordeal took its toll on everyone in the company. We recognized that everyone was affected, particularly the spouses. Many employees thought we were the king and queen. We wanted to show them that we were just like them—real people in real pain." He and Cindy didn't make any speeches; they just talked, sharing everything from Tad's alcoholism to their faith. Their openness had a major effect on the company's employees. The Pipers' vulnerability gave the employees permission to be vulnerable, too. And that became a turning point for the organization.

Tad recalls, "When I was an alcoholic, I typically retreated to a lonely place, and lonely was not a good place to be. Two years later when the bond fiasco hit, I felt alone with a huge burden that I had to fix. Today, I realize that I was never alone. The Lord was with me as an alcoholic and He was with me through this long ordeal." Tad realizes that if he were still a practicing alcoholic when this recent ordeal occurred, it would have been all over for him and Piper Jaffray Companies.

Looking back, Tad says he can see clearly how God was with him. All along Tad was surrounded by people who cared, even though at the time he couldn't see it. His wife Cindy lovingly stood by him through both ordeals, and his friends and associates were there for him, too. Says Tad, "My advice to others is to listen to those who love you. Take a risk, be vulnerable, find a place to go to help you deal with the loneliness."

In 1999, Tad gave a speech to 300 corporate executives in Minneapolis. In his closing remarks, he spoke openly about his ordeal. "My Partner (with the big P) and I work well together, at least when I am paying attention. I find myself looking for joy in every single day and feel able to find it, and feel blessed to be part of His world. I would like to close with a familiar prayer: 'God grant me the serenity to accept the things I cannot change, the courage to change the things I can, and the wisdom to know the difference.' Thy will, not mine, be done."

How did this chapter in Tad's life end? Rising from the depths of destruction, Piper Jaffray became a highly successful $800 million company and in 1997 was sold to U.S. Bancorp, a large regional financial services firm. In 2003, U.S. Bancorp spun off Piper Jaffray, so it once again became an independent entity.

It's no coincidence that Tad's turning point came in the dark of night, while lying in bed. Flat on his back, he no longer saw the storm of problems that surrounded him. Instead, he had the privilege of looking up and seeing that God was with him in the storm. Tad may have lost sight of God in the midst of his problems, but God never lost sight of Tad. He was never alone.

JIM SECORD
"Cooperating with Uncertainty"

Jim Secord is no stranger to change. As former president and CEO of Lakewood Publications and winner of the Hedley Donovan Award for his contributions to the magazine industry, he steered his organization through the turbulence of being sold three times in less than sixteen months. Lakewood Publications flourished, immediately experiencing two of the most profitable years in the company's history.

It was up to Jim to help Lakewood's employees deal with the trauma of uncertainty. He knew that significant change always takes its toll and can be exhausting. And he was not immune to its effect, either.

Jim had learned all about that when Lakewood had a significant layoff. Unfortunately, it was handled poorly. There wasn't much compassion shown in cutting jobs. This created bad feelings for Lakewood's employees, ranging from anger to anxiety. For Jim, not being in control of the circumstances resulted in tremendous stress. He recalls, "I was president at the time and I ended up in the hospital with acute pericarditis. I thought I was having a heart attack. I remember going to the CEO and stating, 'This will never happen again. It's too painful for everyone.'" Because of that time, Jim changed the way he deals with uncertainty and relates to people. He decided that the best way is to help people through change, creating as little trauma and pain as possible.

Jim's lesson taught him not to resist the unknown of change, but to manage it with courage and compassion. He explains that even though the pain cannot always be avoided, it can be managed so a company doesn't lose its most important asset: a committed staff.

Jim identified four principles that helped Lakewood's 100 employees remain focused and committed during this sixteen-month period of change:

A Shared Vision of Success Based on Shared Values

Since 1994, Lakewood has had a vision statement in place that underscores trust, integrity, dignity, and open communication. It was hammered out over a two-year period, during which all 100 employees were asked to participate. More than 450 inputs were gathered through interviews, questionnaires, and the use of an organizational development consultant. "We argued things through and reexamined the company," Jim explains. "The shared vision was the glue that kept us together during the turbulence—it was our benchmark, our guidepost, and a piece of hope."

Open Communication

"Open communication was the antidote to crippling change," declares Jim. "In those sixteen months, even though we were deeply involved in the transactions, we managed to hold six company-wide meetings and we 'memoed' people to death, just to reassure them and keep them posted." Because of the air of uncertainty, Jim made it a point to walk the floor as much as possible, sitting on the corners of people's desks and asking, "What questions do you have? Let me hear what's on your mind."

Nothing was held back. Even the financial information and selling presentation were made available to the employees, the same as was given to potential buyers. Jim recalls, "Communication is a conscious act. It was also a part of who we were as a culture. It was important not only to communicate with them honestly, but also to ask how they were feeling and let them express their fears, so we could address their concerns."

Personal Integrity

"As leaders, we are the role models—that's our charge," says Jim. "The associates looked to me to see how I behaved in difficult circumstances. That's where the trust comes in."

Personal integrity builds trust. During the third sale, the new company offered Jim a "stay bonus" of $75,000 for continuing with the company through the transition. Instead, Jim decided to share his bonus equally with all full-time employees who stayed through the sale. "My philosophy was that we were all in this together, so the decision was easy. It was the right thing to do."

Preparation for Gut-Wrenching Change

At a meeting in New York with Lakewood's new owners, Jim heard the words he most dreaded. "Jim, we're not going to be able to keep the financial department." He winced as he thought of letting twelve loyal employees go. As painful as it was, he knew he had to conduct the process with as much dignity and respect as possible.

Jim's pain is still evident as he tells of that experience. "The most difficult time I can recall was when I needed to get in front of my associates after they stuck with the mission and tell them it was necessary to cut twelve people," he recalls. "I knew they would be upset, but I remember preparing them for change and that this was one of the unfortunate realities of change. I told them it was okay to be angry, to grieve, and that we would help them work through it. I told them we would do whatever we could to help them transition to other jobs. Looking back at that time, everything turned out very well. No one ever came back to us and said that we lied to them or didn't tell them the truth."

As Jim and I were wrapping up, our conversation took an unexpected turn—showing how prophetic his comments about preparing for gut-wrenching change really were. As we prepared to end the interview, I glanced at a beautiful bouquet of flowers on Jim's desk. "Where did you get the flowers?" I asked. Jim smiled as he explained, "Oh, they're from my wife, D'Arcy. She always does things like that." Jim then shared with me that D'Arcy, at the age of fifty-eight, was battling Alzheimer's disease.

"In everyone's life we come to forks in the road. It's not something we want, but it's there. We're then faced with decisions. I could get the best care for D'Arcy and go on with my job. Instead, I have elected to leave the company to be with her. I want to be in a new relationship with her; a new way to love. I haven't figured all the ways to do that, but I will do it and we will walk this journey together. D'Arcy may not understand the same kind of journey when I communicate with her. I may not be speaking to her cognitive mind, but I will be talking to her spiritually. I really believe that God has a purpose in this. D'Arcy is giving to me and to others in her own special way and I'm trying to find out what that is. Also, this is my opportunity to give in a whole new way."

Even though Jim was with the company for thirty-seven years, he says the decision to leave was easy. "I see this situation as a pretty amazing gift," he says. "Once again, I find myself facing uncertainty. In the case of D'Arcy, this situation is much more uncertain than the trauma of the three changes in company ownership. I always felt we would pull through and have a positive outcome with the company changes. With D'Arcy, I feel like I'm going into completely uncharted waters. It's extremely tough, yet I firmly believe this will turn into a potentially magnificent journey."

CONCLUSION

Each leader reaches a point in his or her life where he or she has to ask, "Who's in charge here?" Harry Truman coined the phrase, "The buck stops here," implying that the leader is the one in control, the one with the final responsibility. However, Tad and Jim show us even though leaders are responsible for and accountable to do the things in their power, they are not responsible for, nor can they control, certain outcomes. No matter how experienced and powerful a leader is, there are some things a person has absolutely no control over. This is a very difficult message for most leaders to grasp, as the corporate world supports a leader who is in control and in charge. In the business world, surrender is associated with defeat. In the spiritual realm, however, relinquishing control to God's plan is victory.

To understand why surrender means victory, we need to define surrender. The dictionary gives two distinct definitions. One definition is to give up or to quit; the other is to yield to another's power. The kind of surrender we are speaking of doesn't mean quitting or giving up. It does mean yielding our need to be in control to a much higher authority. Surrender provides us with victory because we are free from the anguish, fear, and guilt that is associated with trying to hold on to something we have no control over. It means we will be at peace, knowing that God is ultimately in charge.

Tad Piper had to come to a place where he could admit he simply couldn't handle the burden of his problem anymore. He finally admitted he was not in control. He started to live again the moment he realized he wasn't alone, when he turned to God and said, "Lord, I can't do it, so you have to."

Jim Secord moved into the most uncertain time in his life. He admitted that it is extremely tough to deal with his wife's Alzheimer's, yet he approaches the experience as a "potentially magnificent journey." He cooperates with uncertainty, not knowing the outcome, but knowing that God is in charge of the situation.

When we are challenged by a need for control, we can choose to view our relationship with God as a partnership rather than as one of a boss and subordinate. Our goal is to walk with God one moment, one day at a time. Dale Carnegie called this living in "day-tight compartments." Quite simply, we have no control over yesterday and no control of tomorrow. We can only do those things within our control today. When we wake up in the morning, we can review the most important issues pressing in that day. Then we prioritize and divide these responsibilities into two categories: things within my control that I will do today, and things outside my control that I will give to God today. Finally, we just work all the things that are within our authority to do.

If we live the day knowing God has a plan for our lives and is in control of all our circumstances, we can learn to cooperate with the uncertainty of a sale, job promotion, or other change by performing the tasks we have in front of us. The uncertainty cannot rob us of the importance of the moment.

DISCUSSION GUIDE

1. What specifically is out of your control, yet causes you worry?
2. What are the things within your control that you can do today?
3. What things can you relinquish and put in God's hands?
4. What things can you do to cooperate with uncertainty?

7

Servant Leadership

From getting the most out of employees
to bringing out the best in employees

*Whoever wants to become great among you must be your servant,
and whoever wants to be first must be slave to all. For even the
Son of Man did not come to be served, but to serve.*

—Mark 10:43–45

Issue:

How do I attract, retain, and motivate good employees?

The meeting started as usual when the general manager's assistant broke in with the dreaded statement: "Corporate's on line one." Immediately, the general manager picked up the phone. The executive committee watched as his face became ashen. We all braced ourselves for the inevitable bad news. After hanging up, he looked up and blurted, "Cut your payroll by 15 percent! I don't care how you do it—just do it! If we don't make budget by June, we'll all be out on the streets!"

At a time when customer service was named a priority, we fired a good percentage of our workforce. It was a disaster. Employee morale was at an all-time low, and, as a result, customer service and our second-quarter profits suffered. The employees who remained eventually cracked under the pressure. At least the corporate office kept their promise: They fired the entire executive committee. I remember us blaming the economy, the competition, and the tough labor market for our fate. We never looked at ourselves.

As we were pressured to meet a tough bottom line, we placed demands on our employees to achieve more with less. Meanwhile, the more we looked to our employees to embrace customer service, the tougher it became to find and retain good employees who were up to the task. Then again, why would an employee want to work in a culture where there was no loyalty, respect, or trust?

Solution:

Serve employees so they can serve others.

Many leaders inadvertently use employees as a means to increase profits. This subtle and misguided intent sends signals to the employee that "we care more about the customer than we care about you," and "we care more about profits than we care about you." God defines a leader as one who serves others, not one who uses others. When we serve others, we help them succeed and, by doing so, communicate, "I care more about you than profits" to our employees and customers. The result is loyal employees and long-standing customers.

In this chapter, we will meet leaders in two different industries: Ken Melrose, retired chairman and CEO of The Toro Company, and Horst Schulze, former president and COO of the Ritz-Carlton Hotel Company. Although they have different personal styles, they've each created an organization that has attracted and kept employees who embrace service. Their solution? Servant leadership. Ken's leadership style promotes a culture of trust. Horst's leadership promotes a culture of dignity and respect. Their servant leadership has created environments to which employees are drawn and in which they thrive. The bottom line? Increased employee retention and solid profitability.

KEN MELROSE
"From Profits First to People First"

Ken Melrose, retired chairman and CEO of The Toro Company, felt very alone as a leader in the 1970s. His focus was different from the typical 1970s leader. He cared deeply about employees, but the popular management theory of the time focused more on profitability. Ken recognized a significant disparity between what he believed in church on Sunday and how he and his coworkers behaved on Monday. He recalls, "I felt called to change the way I behaved in the workplace, and, as a leader, I felt compelled to influence the way others treated one another also."

"It was uncomfortable and awkward at the very least to communicate the biblical principles of servant leadership at a time when talking about God was taboo," Ken explains. "However, the Christian model is to put yourself in awkward and uncomfortable positions and just have faith that God is leading you where He wants you to go." Ken took some risks, like starting a leadership group at Toro that incorporated biblical principles on decision making, power, and hierarchy. The group discussed different ways to make decisions that impact the bottom line, but that also value people and are honest and ethical. Ken's visibility, which started out quiet and subdued, became more prominent, and, as a result, the company did well.

When Ken became CEO of Toro, a manufacturer of home lawn care and turf management products including mowers, aerators, and irrigation systems, it was already a market leader. However, he inherited a culture in which employees were used as a means to get results, and management did whatever it took to achieve the bottom line.

Remarkably, Ken transformed a traditional, bottom-line company into a successful Fortune 500 firm with a turnover rate less that half the national average. His story describes how a leader can integrate employee needs and profit obligations into win-win solutions.

A New Leadership Philosophy—From "Profits First" to "People First"

When Ken became CEO, he deliberately set out to redefine the corporate culture from a "profits first" to a "people first" mentality. Ken knew in his heart that maximizing the potential of his employees would eventually translate to bottom-line success. As he writes in his book, *Making the Grass Greener on Your Side*, "My personal philosophy is this: everyone has the potential to contribute to achieving the goals of the company. If you can unleash that potential, market leadership and financial success will be natural byproducts."[1]

Ken explains that Toro decided to build a business philosophy that focused on putting the employee first. "If you take care of your employees, and eliminate obstacles and barriers to their success," says Ken, "then you will be in a better position to satisfy the customer. And if you satisfy the customer, you will obtain market leadership. And market leadership helps contribute to being an economically healthy and profitable company."

A new philosophy statement was the first step toward changing Toro's culture. The statement served a dual purpose: It communicated a new way of achieving business success, and it provided a blueprint for all employees to be included in the process. The statement reads as follows:

> We believe the single most important factor that influences our success as a company is the Toro employee. There-

fore, it is our privilege and responsibility to create a culture and an environment that supports and encourages individuals at Toro to achieve their highest potential. In order for employees to achieve that potential, we accept the responsibility to show by our actions that we care about them as individuals, understand their needs, recognize their talents, and support them in their efforts to grow and change. At the same time, all of us employees must accept responsibility for our own performance and foster the environment that facilitates this accountability.

As a company, and as the people of Toro, we pledge to execute this philosophy genuinely and with excellence. By doing so, we believe that Toro will be most successful in meeting its overall corporate goals.[2]

This document became the standard for the organization's behaviors and decisions.

A New Leadership Style—Servant Leadership

After stating their new business philosophy, Ken knew that they needed to find a way to execute it. "We needed to find a realistic way to back up our rhetoric," he explains. Ken and his executive team asked themselves, "What kind of leadership style allows the employee to be his or her potential best?"

They began by looking for a leadership idea that enhanced the productivity of Toro's employees. "Servant leadership came about partly from my Christian beliefs and partly because our executive team knew our employees could do their jobs better than we could do them, and it made sense to empower and involve them in the process of growing our business," explains Ken.

A Leadership Challenge—Helping Leaders Change

Next came the toughest challenge: teaching leaders and managers to serve employees. It was clear that leadership and middle management had the primary role of unleashing the potential of employees, but how does a leader significantly influence the behavior of managers who have been rewarded for directing and controlling employees for years? How should they be retrained? How were they to be evaluated? On the bottom line or on employee growth?

Ken found the answer by studying the leadership attributes of Jesus. "If you were to study Christ as a business leader, you would discover the leadership skills needed in business today," says Ken. "Being visionary, being a good communicator, having good listening skills, and motivating people."

Ken found that the best way to train his leaders and managers was by example. His inspiration to demonstrate servant leadership came from learning how Jesus washed the feet of his disciples. "As the leader," Ken explains, "I focus on visible ways of walking the talk as a means to influence leaders and managers. As an example, our officers and directors will periodically walk around the corporate offices serving coffee and donuts, or we will visit our plants and work side-by-side with the workers assembling and building components. In fact, we try to show our vulnerability by demonstrating that we can't do the job as well as the person who owns the job." Ken recognized that demonstrating servant leadership wasn't enough, however. He had to create ways to back up his examples with more widespread action. He didn't want lip service; he wanted people to use servant leadership to solve difficult dilemmas.

One major challenge for leaders and managers was their obligation to both serve employees and make a profit. They saw this as an either/or dilemma and tried to find a balance between profit and people. Instead, Ken challenged his managers to integrate results and relationships into win-win solutions. "The more you tenaciously persevere in integrating these two sides, the better you get as a leader," he affirms.

One example of a people-versus-profits dilemma occurred at a plant in Shakopee, Minnesota, that was faced with seasonal business swings. Toro management struggled with the idea of laying off the plant's employees. Coincidentally, the company was having a problem with a product in the field at the same time. Leaders decided to temporarily move the plant's employees into the field to help distributors solve the problem. These employees went out into the parks and golf courses and worked directly with Toro's customers. This alternative was a win-win solution for everyone: Toro's customers were happy, the employees not only continued to work but also received a great learning experience, and the decision was a profitable one.

To reinforce the new servant-leadership approach, the company developed a new performance appraisal system and modified financial rewards to align with the new corporate philosophy and values. Helping others succeed became an important measure of success. A large portion of senior managers' incentive compensation was changed to reflect how well they practiced the Toro philosophy, as judged by their peers and subordinates.

As behavior began to change, the benefits of servant leadership started to filter through The Toro Company, from leaders to middle managers to employees. Ken explains, "I try to demonstrate leadership in a way that models the expected behaviors so that other leaders are encouraged to do the same thing with their staff, and this cascades throughout the organizational structure. What you end up with is managers not trying to direct and control their people, but trying to coach and serve their people to be more motivated and empowered, and to get better and better in what they do."

When Ken is asked to identify the one thing that has made the most difference over the past twenty years, he names trust.

He believes that creating an environment where people trust each other is one of the most important aspects of servant leadership and one that gives bottom-line results. "People in a trusting environment will stand up and say, 'You can count on me.' It creates a bias for action. It allows the employee to take risks and actions to do what is right," Ken says.

The Payoff—Employee Retention

Ken's leadership philosophy resulted in a dramatic cultural change and unprecedented growth. After twenty years of perseverance and commitment to servant leadership, in 1998 Toro enjoyed a turnover ratio that was less than half the national average. Since then, Toro's turnover ratio has remained low.

"Why do Toro's employees want to work for the company?" Ken offers. "Most people want to value other people and produce quality work. They want to work in an environment that values trust and respect. They want to work for someone who is trustworthy, where they can take a risk and not get hammered, and be accountable without having to fear getting burned. There is great potential in all of Toro's employees to do quality work if they're allowed to."

Ken's leadership is based on three key attributes: faith, courage, and perseverance. His faith created a calling and conviction to live godly principles at a time when it was uncommon. His courage enabled him to take risks by teaching servant leadership at a time when it went completely against contemporary leadership theory. His perseverance helped him to build a successful Fortune 500 company with more than 4,800 employees where people were respected and appreciated, and profits remained solid. And even though he retired in 2005 (though remaining on the board of directors as chairman), through his faith-based philosophy Ken and Toro have continued to realize the fruits of his labor.

HORST SCHULZE
"An Uncompromising Respect for People"

It's clear where Horst Schulze's passion lies. He has an uncompromising respect for people, borne out of his love for God. Horst honors a basic biblical principle: By enhancing employees' self-worth and dignity, he enhances their ability to provide exceptional service to their customers. This core value, providing respect and dignity for every human being, helped Ritz-Carlton, of which he was founding president, COO, and vice chairman (leaving in 2002), become one of the most successful hotel chains in the world.

"We are ladies and gentlemen serving ladies and gentlemen." The Ritz-Carlton motto defines how the company values each employee, as well as the service those employees provide to their customers. This principle works. Whereas the standard hospitality industry employee turnover rate is in excess of 100 percent per year, the Ritz-Carlton Hotel Company boasts a turnover rate of only 29 percent. It was the first hospitality organization to receive the Malcolm Baldridge National Quality Award. Ritz-Carlton remains an outstanding success story and an industry leader in employee satisfaction, customer satisfaction, and profitability.

But Horst's servant leadership isn't soft. A leader who cares about people doesn't have to care less about the bottom line. Horst is a demanding leader who sets high standards of excellence, quality, and service. During his tenure at Ritz-Carlton, as well as his other positions within the service industry, he expected the company to be regarded as the quality and market leader in the hotel industry. Horst explains, "When making decisions, I ask myself: Is it good for all concerned—God, the organization, the employees, the customers, and vendors? If yes, then drive it forward relentlessly."

Horst set the standard for an equal commitment to respect and dignity from every employee in the Ritz-Carlton organization. "I demand from every manager that every employee be respected fully as a human being," he said at the time. "I make it very clear that no one can claim to be a better human being than another. A dishwasher is as important in this organization as a vice president."

The key to Horst's success in all the companies for which he's worked lies in how he weaves biblical principles and values, including respect, caring, trust, fairness, and teamwork, into the fabric of his organizations. These values and principles were the foundation for Ritz-Carlton's success, as measured by employee retention, customer satisfaction, and profitability.

The concluding paragraph of the Ritz-Carlton mission statement reads:

> We will always select employees who share our values. We will strive to meet individual needs because our success depends on the satisfaction, effort, and commitment of each employee. Our leaders will constantly support and energize all employees to continuously improve productivity and customer satisfaction. This will be accomplished by creating an environment of genuine care, trust, respect, fairness, and teamwork through training, education, empowerment, participation, recognition, rewards, and career opportunities.

Horst and Ritz-Carlton leadership created a system that enables every employee to connect with the organization's core values in a powerful and meaningful way. Four primary components, including the employee selection process, involved leadership, training and education, and daily communication, have turned these values and goals into a living reality.

The Employee Selection Process

Horst explains that Ritz-Carlton takes the time to select the right people for the right job and doesn't hire someone just to fill a position. "Our industry is notorious for getting bodies to fulfill a function—do things," he says. "I think it is irresponsible and in a sense immoral. People should not just fulfill a function. They have a right to be a part of something."

Ritz-Carlton uses a highly sophisticated process to determine the character traits needed to fulfill a particular position, as well as to determine the ability of a candidate to meet the specific job requirements. In essence, the company takes a painstaking amount of effort to see if there is both a competency and values fit. Horst explains, "There needs to be the right fit for the employee and the organization. The same is true with our values. It is important that the employee believes in the same values as we do."

This up-front effort produced enormous back-end results. Incorporation of this selection process alone contributed to a 50 percent drop in Ritz-Carlton's turnover rate.

Involved Leadership

Horst Schulze demands a lot from himself and his fellow leaders. He tells people, "Leadership sets the vision, the standards, the values, and goals of the organization, and then we caringly involve every single employee in the process. We do that by living the values—sharing them slowly, carefully, and properly."

Leadership's role, Horst insists, is to "support and energize" employees to continuously improve productivity and customer satisfaction. This is done by demonstrating the values and modeling the correct way. At Ritz-Carlton, it is every manager's responsibility to work side by side with his or her employees.

When opening a new hotel, Horst personally communicated the organization's values. "Every hotel we have opened, I have opened," he said. "I have helped train the maids, the waiters, and so on. I stayed for ten days so they knew that I was there to be with them. And I told them, 'Yes, I'm important,' and then I pointed to each and every employee and said, 'but so are you, and you, and you.'"

Training and Education

Ritz-Carlton provides more than 100 hours of training and education to each employee. The focus of this training is on the company's core values. "It is critical that the values are clearly understood by everyone," explains Horst. The organization has developed "Our Gold Standards," which clearly define the vision, values, goals, and methodology of Ritz-Carlton. These Gold Standards include:

- **The Credo:** reinforces the priority and commitment toward service
- **The Three Steps to Service:** further define the specific activities and decisions of customer interface
- **The Ritz-Carlton Basics:** twenty points that focus entirely on guest problem-solving and help eliminate internal competition
- **The Ritz-Carlton Motto:** reinforces the values of respect, dignity, and service

Daily Communication

"We created a system that reinforces the company's values to every one of its 16,000 employees every single day," explains Horst. Ritz-Carlton has a daily program called the line-up. Every day, for every shift, an employee meeting is held that provides an opportunity for employees to communicate, from getting instructions for the day to solving problems. In addition to the necessary communication that takes place at the hotel level, the corporate office sends out a daily message that reinforces their goals and values. These messages help the employees grow, personally and professionally. "For example," says Horst, "a message will pass on congratulations to specific employees on anniversary dates, or they will provide tips on dealing with stress, or provide an inspirational quote of the day."

Horst Schulze turned his uncompromising respect for people into a successful culture. His servant leadership, with its focus on biblical principles and values, helped make the Ritz-Carlton Hotel Company a worldwide leader.

CONCLUSION

While the business world commonly attempts to address employee attraction and retention issues by implementing hit-or-miss programs, that's not the solution. The solution to the issue of attracting and retaining employees who embrace the model of service is a paradigm shift in our definition of leadership.

The customer service and organizational commitment of your employees is directly influenced by your definition of leadership. The business world commonly defines a leader as being one of the most powerful and influential persons in an organization. In other words, a leader is first among many. Being amongst the most powerful in an organization, a leader's job includes directing others.

The Bible says "whoever wants to become great among you must be your servant, and whoever wants to be first must be slave of all. For even the Son of Man did not come to be served, but to serve" (Mark 10:43–45). God clearly states that a leader puts the needs of all others before his own needs. Instead of directing others, God defines a leader as one who serves others.

Servant leadership became a business term during the 1970s, when Robert Greenleaf coined the phrase "servant-leader." He defined the servant-leader as one who is a servant first, a leader who desires to make sure other people's needs are being served. At first glance, being a servant-leader is contradictory to success in a highly competitive, bottom-line world, but servant leadership is the tool God gave leaders to succeed. Everything God designs is a perfect and trustworthy blueprint for success.

ACNielsen, a market research and analysis firm, has conducted regular employee surveys and linked the results with customer satisfaction data. The company has found that when employee satisfaction rises, financial results improve. A financial services unit at Monsanto conducted baseline customer and employee satisfaction surveys. They found that employee satisfaction with work/life balance and general job satisfaction were the two strongest predictors of customer satisfaction.[3]

Ken Melrose and Horst Schulze are very different leaders. They come from different backgrounds, work in diverse industries, and have different personal styles and approaches to servant leadership. Ken boldly spun Toro's culture on its head by prioritizing people over profits, and Horst raised the standard of service of Ritz-Carlton employees. Regardless of approach, style, and industry, they were each business successes because they found a way to bring out the best in their employees. As a result, each of their organizations has enjoyed the benefits of low employee turnover, increased customer satisfaction, and long-term growth and profitability.

These men and their organizations share some commonalities:

- While their source of inspiration is found in their faith in God, they were able to communicate the core principles to their workforce in a meaningful and nonthreatening way.
- Each leader demonstrated the values of respect, integrity, and service through leadership by example.
- The importance of these core principles was demonstrated through the commitment of time, energy, training, and money.
- Ken and Horst each said that helping the employee succeed was the key to customer service and business success. They backed this philosophy with action.
- They created atmospheres that equipped and enabled the employee to succeed, whether it was in the selection process, training, or the environment.
- Their internal systems were based on a long-term process, not a short-term program.
- For Toro and Ritz-Carlton, servant leadership has worked. Employees are attracted and retained, customers are satisfied, and the companies are profitable.

As servant leaders, we can reinforce the employee behaviors that honor the organization's philosophy by creating a daily focus on the four R's.

1. **Resources:** Identify the resources needed to maximize employee performance. Resources can include training, technical support, and financial support, among others. Identification of needed resources starts by asking employees what they need to do their jobs better.

2. **Respect:** Respect begins with recognizing the employee as a unique individual rather than a body filling a job. As we have seen from the case studies, finding both the right skills fit and the right values fit is a very important piece to employee retention. Consistent communication between leadership and employees is essential for a continued partnership between organization and employee.

3. **Recognition:** Recognition for a job well done is one of the greatest reinforcements for good behavior. Even better, recognition can be free. Most employees desire acknowledgment for their contributions. Create a daily plan to recognize contributions. This will motivate the employee and help shape the behavior we desire.

4. **Reward:** The best way to reward employees is to ask them how they like to be rewarded. Remember, everyone is different. Some people like to be recognized publicly, some privately. Have each employee identify small tangible rewards (food, gift certificates, plaques) and intangible rewards (pat on the back, verbal praise) and create ways to celebrate individual and team victories along the way.

Servant leadership is the key to attracting, retaining, and motivating good employees. Leaders who create an environment that appreciates employee talent, helps them grow, and brings out their best, will, like Ken Melrose and Horst Schulze, reap the reward of loyal, long-term employees. Serving the servant will help your employees and your organization succeed.

DISCUSSION GUIDE

1. How do you define the quality and integrity of "service" in your organization?

2. How do you define servant leadership?

3. How would you define your leadership role?

4. What is your toughest challenge when it comes to finding and keeping employees?

5. Identify the most important lesson you learned from the two case studies.

6. Identify one action you will take to improve employee satisfaction.

7. Identify one action you will take to improve the level of service in your organization.

Notes

1. Karen Lund, "Owners at Every Corner," *Minnesota Business & Opportunities* (August 1997).

2. Sue Shellenberger, "Surveys Link Satisfaction of Employees, Customers," *Wall Street Journal* as published by *Star Tribune* (January 25, 1999).

3. Ibid.

8

Love

From love *or* the bottom line to love *and* the bottom line

Love is patient, love is kind. It does not envy, it does not boast, it is not proud. It is not rude, it is not self-seeking, it is not easily angered, it keeps no record of wrongs. Love does not delight in evil but rejoices with the truth. It always protects, always trusts, always hopes, always perseveres.

—1 Corinthians 13:4–7

Issue:

How do I balance the needs of others with my profit obligations?

David and Sarah faced a difficult dilemma. David had received an excellent job offer with a substantial pay increase in Florida. However, he and his family lived in Minnesota, close to extended family and a school in which his son was academically and socially thriving. It was clear that moving out of Minnesota was not in the best interest of the family, even though the increase in salary would be sorely welcome. David and Sarah agreed that the opportunity could benefit the family greatly. While the decision was difficult, David accepted the job offer, moving to Florida for one year; he traveled back to Minnesota every other weekend to be with his family.

John was a servant-leader who deeply cared for his eighty employees. When the company he worked for sold his division to a larger, bottom line–driven company, the acquiring company demanded that he eliminate twenty jobs, cutting his staff by a quarter. He didn't want to work for this organization with differing values or let go of twenty employees he cared about. Confronted with a seemingly lose-lose dilemma, in frustration he resigned.

Solution:

Change your focus from "Love *or* the Bottom Line" to "Love *and* the Bottom Line."

L eading with love and achieving a company's bottom line appear to be conflicting goals. The work/family balance dilemma, for example, remains a frontline issue—for both employees and companies alike. We feel pulled in opposite directions: loving others on one side and working to achieve financial goals on the other. Is there a solution to this values tug of war?

Joel Manby, President and CEO of Herschend Family Entertainment Corporation, and Cheryl Bachelder, CEO of Popeyes Louisiana Kitchen, Inc., have transformed the "Love *or* the bottom line" mentality into the revolutionary "Love *and* the bottom line."

"Some people think leadership is only about the bottom line," explains Joel. "Leadership is about the bottom line *and* loving the people you work with, making your community a better place, feeling a sense of satisfaction at the end of the day, and leading employees who can't imagine working anywhere else. These things aren't mutually exclusive. In fact, the opposite is true: The bottom line is best served when leaders lead with love."[1]

The case studies of these two successful CEOs are hope-filled. Leading with love not only adds to the bottom line; it contributes to a company's much greater purpose.

JOEL MANBY
"Love Works"

Joel Manby is an American success story. As a young boy, Joel was determined to rise above his circumstances and find prosperity. His dad, owner of a small farm machinery dealership in Battle Creek, Michigan, struggled to keep food on the table. "Growing up without financial means, I didn't want the same financial pressures of my parents," Joel explains. He worked hard, became a straight-A student, and graduated from Harvard Business School. As an executive at Saturn Corporation, he helped the startup carmaker go from zero to $5 billion a year in revenue in just three years. His success at Saturn resulted in a promotion to CEO of Saab North America, where he led the division to its second-best year in Saab's North American history.

"My wife, Marki, and I moved ten times in fifteen years as I accepted new leadership positions of increasing responsibility and pressure. The constant moving put a tremendous strain on our home life and our four girls. I spent more than 250 days on the road, mostly in Asia—and even when I was home, I consistently had 6:00 A.M. phone calls with Sweden and 11:00 P.M. phone calls with the Asian markets.

"On September 13, 1999, I was in Australia for a Saab distributor meeting and called Marki to catch up. As she started to talk, her voice cracked. 'This is the second year in a row you've been away on my birthday. When you're home, you're not really *home*. This is not what I signed up for. I thought I could handle this, and I've tried. But this isn't working for our family. You're frustrated. You're not happy, and neither am I. The kids don't really know you. Something needs to change.'"[2]

Marki's words were a wake-up call. Joel deeply desired to be a good husband and father. So he went to his boss, the CEO of Saab worldwide, to ask if he could return to "only" being CEO of Saab's North American Operations, a move that would cut Joel's travel in half. His boss refused.[3]

Joel made the difficult decision to leave Saab and soon accepted a position as CEO of a startup company in California. In his first week, the NASDAQ crashed, losing over a third of its value. Joel began working 24/7 to try and salvage the company. He rented an apartment in California and was able to travel back home to Atlanta only once or twice a month.

The path he thought would lead him back to his family instead had led him to a bare, lonely apartment. One rainy night, depressed and hopeless, Joel wrestled with some serious questions. *My entire career I've been so driven . . . for what? Is there any hope of balancing my career goals with my family goals? Are quarterly profit reports really what life is all about?*[4]

"My cell phone rang. It was Jack Herschend, chairman of Herschend Family Entertainment Corporation (HFE), one of the largest themed entertainment companies in the world. I had been on the board of HFE for three years and thought very highly of Jack and the company."

"Joel, how are you brother?" he asked.

"His compassionate nature opened the floodgates of my emotion as I shared my situation. What he said next surprised me. 'I'm retiring as chairman next year and all of us on the board would like you to be the next chairman of HFE. Would you consider it?'"[5]

What Joel didn't know then was that Jack Herschend's offer would revolutionize his view of leadership and the bottom line. Joining HFE as chairman and CEO, Joel found a successful and profitable business where the bottom line was essential. But there was more.

"Leadership is about the bottom line *and . . .*" Joel discovered ". . . and loving the people you work with, and making your community a better place, and feeling a sense of satisfaction at the end of every day, and leading employees who can't imagine working anywhere else. The bottom line is best served when leaders lead with love."[6]

In his final board meeting at HFE, Jack Herschend shared these words: "It's important that the board and the leadership never lose sight of the three main Herschend family objectives: a specified growth in profit so it is 'a great long-term investment'; to be a 'great place to work for great people'; and to 'lead with love.' We understand that sometimes tension can exist between these objectives, but that is a tension that needs to be managed. It's not okay to achieve profit growth and destroy our culture as a 'great place to work for great people.' It is also not okay to focus on being a 'great place to work' without achieving our financial objectives. This is a tension to *embrace*, not eliminate."[7]

Several years later, Joel is now convinced that leading with love is the best way to run an organization. *Any organization.*[8]

Joel is quick to clarify his definition, as he understands how easily the word *love* is misunderstood and misused. "Love isn't a feeling, but an action." At HFE, the principle of love doesn't force a particular belief system on people, nor does it exclude anyone—regardless of their faith. What it does do is provide freedom for employees to live out their values.

"Agape love is the foundation for the best and noblest relationships that humans are capable of. It is deliberate and unconditional love that is the result of choices and behaviors rather than feelings and emotions."[9]

Joel also understands how the pressure of the bottom line and poor relationships can undermine business cultures. Healthy relationships, he claims, are the key to results. "Agape love will promote healthy relationships among employees and their leaders, allowing people to perform at their very best, all the while withstanding the pressure and tension that can exist within a high-performance organization. Agape love is a leadership principle that holds leaders accountable and helps any organization become healthier and more enthusiastic."[10]

In his book, *Love Works*, Joel identifies seven leadership principles, paraphrased from 1 Corinthians 13:4–7: "Love is patient, love is kind. It does not envy, it does not boast, it is not proud. It is not rude, it is not self-seeking, it is not easily angered, it keeps no record of wrongs. Love does not delight in evil but rejoices with the truth. It always protects, always trusts, always hopes, always perseveres."

Joel explains, "These are principles that will transform your organization, from the bottom line to the bottom of your employees' hearts. Love is . . .

- Patient
- Kind
- Trusting
- Unselfish
- Truthful
- Forgiving
- Dedicated"[11]

How does HFE communicate biblical principles in a diverse business setting? Joel answers, "We don't need you to believe a certain way, we want you to behave a certain way." Early on, as Joel witnessed love in action through the behaviors of HFE's leaders and employees, he realized, "They didn't call it love, they just behaved that way." He saw the principles of 1 Corinthians 13 working to build healthy attitudes and relationships, the kind that made HFE successful.

Let's take a look at a few of these principles and see how love works at HFE.

Kindness

While most of us would agree that a culture of kindness would be of great benefit to employees and customers alike, why don't we experience more in organizations? Joel answers, "It's hard to execute and it takes unending leadership and focus."

"At HFE, we specifically focus on creating an enthused workforce that treats the end consumer with kindness. All employees (including leaders) are given a kindness rating as part of their annual review, a rating that measures enthusiasm, passion, and encouragement. Kindness isn't an add-on—it's a critical component of any well-run organization. Kindness is the root of encouragement, encouragement leads to enthusiasm, and everyone benefits."[12]

Joel admits it's hard to pause and say "thank you" to others who help make the organization successful. He's improved in this area thanks to his boss. Evidence of Jack Herschend's kindness is everywhere. "As I walk the halls of our park offices, I see notes everywhere from Jack and Peter. They may be framed on walls, taped to the edge of computer monitors, or displayed in scrapbooks, but all are kept because all are special."[13]

In fact, Joel still has two letters he received from Jack. The first came at a time when Joel was in great need of encouragement. In the midst of the 2009 recession, Joel had to make some agonizing decisions. The note read:

"Joel, as you said, '09 has been a tough year and I agree. In some respects it has been a great year in that you and your team have proved that you can manage thru the toughest times you are likely to experience the rest of your career. Thank you for the awesome jacket and the kind words. Jack"

"His note was exactly what I needed. The power of his kind encouragement helped me redouble my efforts to solve our problems and move our company in a positive direction. Jack didn't berate me for what was going wrong—he encouraged me about what was going right."[14]

"Of course, that meant longer hours at the office, more missed family dinners, and more travel. Then, about six months later, Marki also got a handwritten note from Jack."

"Dear Marki, Lauren, Erinn, Jesse, and Anna,

Over the last two days I had the privilege of watching your dad provide the most awesome leadership to the President's team. It was the kind of leadership that leads to actions pleasing to Jesus. I'm soooo grateful you all choose to share him with us.

Appreciatively, Jack"

"I called Jack and asked, 'How do you do it? We're all busy with conflicts and demands on our time, so how do you always seem to write the perfect note at the perfect time?'

"Jack's answer shed light on how to practice kindness. 'I spend the first twenty minutes of my morning reflecting on the day before,' he told me. 'I think about what behavior I saw that should be encouraged, and then I write a note to reinforce it and to say thanks.'"[15]

Unselfish

In many ways, economic difficulty contributes to a survival mentality—both among individuals and organizations. Time is limited and resources are scarce. So how does an organization create a culture of open-handed generosity during tight-fisted times? HFE's leaders believe creating a culture of unselfish giving is the smart thing to do.

Monica was a seasonal employee at Wild Adventures Theme Park in Valdosta, Georgia. Unexpectedly, her sister died, leaving behind Layla, her sister's nine-month-old daughter. Just twenty-one years old and single, Monica decided to adopt Layla as her own. With only a seasonal job at Wild Adventures and parents whose financial resources were limited, Monica was encouraged by HFE to apply for help from the Share It Forward Foundation. The Foundation agreed to help with the costs of her sister's funeral. Further, Monica qualified for a monthly stipend through the single-parent program. As a young woman, Monica made the selfless decision to adopt her sister's baby, and her selflessness was aided by HFE's selflessness. Her story is one of hundreds within HFE each year.[16]

HFE's Share It Forward Foundation is a practical model that assists employees in need. Here's how it works. HFE employees start the momentum with their donations (personal selflessness). Out of profits, the company matches employee donations (organizational unselfishness). Then the Herschend family gives an additional grant. To show his personal commitment, Joel donates 100 percent of the royalties from *Love Works* to this foundation. Nearly 10 percent of HFE's seasonal employees have received some kind of financial assistance through the Foundation and to date, more than 800 families have benefited.[17]

Joel is adamant that programs like Share It Forward don't have a negative impact on corporate financial performance. "In fact, the opposite is true. Foundations like Share It Forward create organization-wide loyalty and passion and help maintain an enthusiastic, motivated workforce and satisfied guests."[18]

As a corporate principle, the significance of selflessness—both personal and organizational—has been infused as love, compassion, and support into 800 grateful families.

Truthful

Getting at the truth is one of the most difficult tasks of leadership. In challenging situations, it's often easier to avoid rather than confront. Whether employees or leaders need to hear the truth, individuals or departments are in conflict, or a poor performer needs to be let go, there's an endless need for sharing the truth. Speaking the truth—in love—is essential in business.

Joel explains how truth is an important part of leadership. Leaders must define the truth of the organization's real role in the marketplace and identify its weaknesses and strengths. Equally, a leader must ensure that the truth is communicated to every individual about his or her performance and how it can be improved. That's why the need for truth is both corporate and individual.[19] Getting at the truth keeps the best people and creates the best decisions.

"Leading with love means caring enough about an individual or a team to give and solicit truthful feedback. When leaders provide their teams with the truth about their performance as well as the tools to be successful, *regardless of personal feelings*, this is a sure sign of leading with love."[20]

Joel uses a simple tool, which can be used for either one-on-one or team communications. On a piece of paper, make three headings and title them "Same as," "More of," and "Less of." Under the "Same as" heading, write down each of the things you appreciate most about the individual. Under the "More of" heading, identify the things you want to see more of from the person. Finally, under "Less of," record the things that are negative and need to be reduced or eliminated. This same approach can be used in a group setting when an entire team is behaving in a dysfunctional manner. As Joel explains, "Speaking the truth isn't always easy, but we can't lead with love unless we love the truth."[21]

Since *God Is My CEO* was first published, the most frequently asked questions remain, "Can I live my faith and be profitable in a bottom-line world?" and "How can I balance employee needs with profit obligations?"

As he stepped away from actively running the company he created, Jack Herschend's message was that the tension between profit growth and leading with love was one to embrace, not eliminate. This continues to be an important and achievable objective, regardless of economic conditions. Joel affirms, "During the past seven years at HFE, we have grown operating profit more than 50 percent and have earned over a 14 percent annual return for our owners, clearly beating the large and small cap stock market performance during very difficult times. And we have done that while consciously leading with love."[22]

Joel Manby and Herschend Family Entertainment illustrate that you can live your faith and lead your organization to financial success. At HFE, Joel discovered that the way to lead the way he wants to lead (his professional life) and live the way he wants to live (his personal life) is a perfect match through the principle of love. Embracing the teaching of Jesus in Matthew 22:37 and 39, "Love the Lord your God with all your heart and with all your soul and with all your mind . . . Love your neighbor as yourself," Joel discovered that love works!

CHERYL BACHELDER
"Remembered and Remarkable Leadership: Leading for the Sake of Others"

Cheryl Bachelder, CEO of Popeyes Louisiana Kitchen, Inc., was in the midst of a speech to fellow business leaders, explaining how servant leadership has contributed to a remarkable 412 percent increase in Popeyes' stock price. With deep passion and sincerity, she blurted out, "We love our franchisees!" Her comment stopped me. *Love our franchisees*? What an odd statement to make in front of business leaders. What did she mean? How does loving franchisees translate to growing your bottom line? So I asked her.

"In October 2001, I was knocked off balance with the diagnosis of stage 1 breast cancer. When you realize your days are numbered, it drives you to reconsider how you're spending your time and, if nothing else, it makes you want to be hugely intentional with the days you have remaining. It made me review my approach to my work life and my family life. I believe passionately that we should have an intentional purpose about our daily lives and it should be obvious to those who know us what we stand for, what we are trying to contribute, and how we intend to be of service to this life because on your last day I think all of us in our heart of hearts hope to have a life of meaning, a life that in some small way made a difference. After my cancer diagnosis, it took a few years of searching before I came to understand my purpose.

"My purpose and passion is clear. It's to develop purpose-driven leaders who exhibit competence and character in all aspects of life. At Popeyes, my purpose is to inspire and develop servant-leaders as a means to delivering exceptional performance results for franchisees, team members, and shareholders."

In an interview with *www.womenetics.com*, Cheryl described how she came to that focused passion. "In my own career I've observed a lot of leaders in large corporate America and, frankly, have been desperately disappointed in the caliber of leaders of my generation, my peer group . . . I have found American leaders self-absorbed and selfish, always focused on getting a bigger jet, more stock, bigger houses. It's all about them. I've observed the impact that (attitude) has on the organization. No one is motivated by your personal ambition—no one cares about your personal ambition. They care about a greater purpose, doing something that matters and working for someone who cares about them.

"I started to wonder what it would be like if you led the way you want to be led, if you were the boss you wanted to work for. It's a fascinating conversation to have with people—asking them to describe the ideal qualities of a boss. They always say, 'They took time with me, took risks with me, they taught me and had my back.' Then I ask, 'Are you that boss to someone today?' Their face freezes because they've never thought about it that way. That's human nature. We're wired to be selfish two-year-olds. But we have to fight our nature and be the boss we want to work for. That's what led me to servant leadership—it's the highest standard." [23]

"For me, Jesus is the absolute best teacher that has ever walked. He selflessly loved people, genuinely cared, and gave dignity to every life. That, to me, is the guidepost that drives servant leadership. I always tell my people, we are not servant-leaders; we're just trying to be servant-leaders. Every day we will bump into ourselves, make mistakes, and fall short of the kind of selfless love demonstrated by Christ. We are not Him, but what an ambition to follow and try to be like Him. I couldn't imagine a higher standard for living one's life."

On Cheryl's website, *www.ThePurposeOfLeadership.com*, she shares the text of a speech she gave on the topic of remembered and remarkable leadership. To be a remembered and remarkable leader, she explains, your leadership purpose must be something greater than your self-interests. You must lead for the sake of others.

"At Popeyes, we are in the middle of a 'Grand Experiment.' We are transforming the leadership culture of the company from a mindset of self-interest (*What do I get?*) to a mindset of service to others (*What do I give?*). We are on a steep, challenging learning curve.

"Our first decision was, 'Who do we serve?' Would we strive to improve our service to our guests? Would we focus on the interests of our shareholders? Would we serve the owners who had invested their life savings in a twenty-year contract to be a Popeyes franchisee?

"Based on my words, you would shout out, well of course, you would choose the franchisee.

"But this is not the norm in our industry. Typically the corporation serves its self-interest, focusing on the guest (which means growing sales) and delivering for the investor (which means getting the share price up). In real life, the franchisee is typically viewed as a complaining, emotional small business owner who is forever challenging the leadership and slowing down progress. Our team decided to challenge conventional thinking and see what would happen if we focused on serving our franchisees as our #1 customer.

"We believed in our hearts that if we took actions that substantially improved their lives and livelihood, all the other stakeholders would be well served . . . our employees, our guests, and our shareholders."[24]

Cheryl agrees with Joel Manby that love is an action verb. "In our business, we have many opportunities to love our business owners and all the people who work in our restaurants. Nearly 60,000 people work in our restaurants around the globe. Every one of those people is an opportunity to express love."

"Recently, we had a very poignant experience where an individual within our company passed away suddenly in his forties, leaving his wife and son. Within hours, a group from our home office and a team of franchise owners took action, putting together a fund of $50,000 to educate this man's son. It just happened because of the values that reside in our company.

"Love isn't soft. It's a performance strategy. We have 300 business owners. One way I demonstrate love is to establish a trusting relationship with them. I listen to them, am in the moment, and give them my time. One business owner felt that his relationship with me deserved special treatment. He asked for preferential financial terms in his business agreement. I explained to him that my role is to treat all franchise owners the same so they can count on me to be fair in all business dealings and never be suspicious of offering preferential treatment. Loving didn't mean giving him what he wanted. Love can be a tough message, whether it be with a business associate or a teenage son or daughter. It's not always a hug or being soft. It has to be the loving thing even if it is difficult news or not the answer you want."

At *www.ThePurposeOfLeadership.com*, Cheryl describes the results of Popeyes' focus on franchisee service. "Five years after deciding to build relationships *with* and results *for* our franchisees, Popeyes' average restaurant sales have increased from $1 million per restaurant to $1.2 million per restaurant, up 20 percent. That sales growth combined with a $36 million cost savings initiative has increased the franchisee's average restaurant profits by 35 percent or $63,000 per restaurant. Our 350 newly opened restaurants now deliver top-tier cash on cash returns to our franchisees, compared to nearly zero returns five years ago."

"The other stakeholders, how did they fare? Our employee engagement is now significantly higher than industry norms. Our guest experience rating of our restaurants has improved 17 percentage points. And our investors have been rewarded by a 412 percent increase in our stock price." [25]

One of the quotes that most inspires Cheryl is from Max Stackhouse, professor at Princeton Theological Seminary, who says, "Increasingly business leaders will be stewards of civilization. We will observe and watch as other institutions fail, the government, the family, the school system, etc. Yet business will find itself in the crosshairs of those changes in civilization with the opportunity to have a positive impact."

In response, Cheryl says, "I see it in our day-to-day business. We practice our business model in every culture, every religious faith, and in every kind of government, whether dictator or democracy. We have an opportunity to teach competencies in business but also character traits and values of business that create environments where people can thrive. That is a huge burden and responsibility placed on business leaders. What kind of business leaders will we be in that moment of opportunity that we're given to establish on this soil or in other countries? How will that be part of our stewardship of civilization going forward? I don't think this is too esoteric a quote for describing what we are being called by God to do. We are called to make a positive difference for people so that they may know a loving God. To me that is the ultimate opportunity for stewardship."

Cheryl Bachelder is a new style of business leader—one that views a servant-leadership model as an opportunity to impact people of every faith, culture, government, and country. As CEO, her job isn't just about the bottom line, but one of positively impacting thousands of lives on a global scale.

CONCLUSION

Love isn't another strategy to achieve business profitability. It's a revolutionary paradigm shift in the way we view leadership. Joel Manby and Cheryl Bachelder are purposeful and intentional leaders who, by leading with love, inspire and motivate others. Do you remember how Joel described leadership? He said, "Leadership is about the bottom line *and* . . . and loving the people you work with, and making your community a better place, and feeling a sense of satisfaction at the end of every day, and leading employees who can't imagine working anywhere else. The bottom line is best served when leaders lead with love."[26]

Love is an action verb. Selflessness is promoted over selfish ambition. Service to others is rewarded over self-serving agendas. Patience, kindness, love, respect, and truthfulness aren't words on a plaque—they're actions and behaviors that are trained, measured, monitored, and reinforced.

Implementing the principles of love may require some soul searching. In the bottom-line world in which we work, leading with love isn't easy. It isn't a fast way to lead, nor is it necessarily an efficient way to lead. Cheryl received a cancer diagnosis and began a several-year leadership journey to discover what matters most before she found her true calling. Joel found clarity after traveling 250 days a year away from his family. Both leaders first thought about the benefits of this approach from the personal, spiritual, and practical business perspectives.

Whatever your leadership approach is, it has both a value and a cost to it—two sides of the same coin, if you will. If your focus is a bottom-line one, you probably have a good feel for the financial value you bring to the company. But have you ever thought about what your leadership approach costs your company? In his books *Built to Last* and *Good to Great*, Jim Collins explains that successful and sustainable companies have the courage and discipline to confront the brutal facts of their business, particularly as it relates to the culture of their organization. Since one of love's action verbs is honesty, I urge you to honestly assess the hidden cost to your business of each of the following threats.

Five Hidden Threats: What's the Cost?

1. **Greed:** Ambition is of great benefit in business, whether it's personal initiative, drive, or determination. When personal ambition becomes selfish ambition, however, greed can creep in—to a company's detriment. Merriam-Webster defines greed as, "A selfish and excessive desire for more of something (as money) than is needed."[27]

    Has your business been negatively impacted by some form of stakeholder (employees, leaders, customers, shareholders) greed? How does owner or shareholder pressure negatively impact your organization's culture?

2. **Dishonesty:** Dishonesty—at any level—damages a business's reputation and costs money. On a company-wide level, the ethicality of a company's business practices impacts buyer decisions to purchase from that company. On an employee level, dishonesty such as employee theft, falsifying time sheets, lying, or harassment costs a company in hard dollars.

    Have you lost business due to the unethical or dishonest practice of someone within your organization? Do you detect a lack of trust from any of your stakeholders? What does leader and employee dishonesty cost your business?

3. **Disengagement:** In "10 Reasons Your Top Talent Will Leave You," *www.forbes.com* reported that more than 70 percent of employees don't feel appreciated or valued by their employer.[28] Undervaluing employees leads to low job satisfaction and disengagement. Even your top tal-

ent will walk out your front door and into a competing organization.

What's the level of employee satisfaction and engagement in your organization? What's the turnover rate? Do you know why employees leave your company? If they're leaving because they feel unappreciated, what's the root cause within your culture?

4. **Differing values:** Forbes' "10 Reasons" article also reported that more than 50 percent of employees say their values differ from those of their employer.[29]

   How have you communicated the vision and values of your company? Do your day-to-day actions align with your communication? Do you know the values of your employees and what values they seek in a leader? Do you have a method to align company values with employee values?

5. **Conflict:** CPP Inc. commissioned a worldwide study on workplace conflict. The 2008 study found that "workplace conflict is rampant throughout the business world, with U.S. employees spending more than 2.8 hours per week dealing with conflict." According to the report, this amounts to approximately $359 billion in hours paid dealing with conflict (based on average U.S. hourly earnings of $17.95). The study also found that 22 percent of employees said that avoiding conflict has led to sickness or absence from work. Perhaps most importantly, the report indicated that *properly managed* conflict can actually benefit an organization.[30]

What is conflict costing your business? What are the conflicts' root causes and how can you help manage and resolve them?

Now that you've assessed the hard dollar costs of leading with a bottom-line focus, let's take a brief look at the flip side—how and why could leading with love revolutionize your business?

Three Clear Benefits of Leading with Love: What's the Value?

1. **Love builds healthy relationships amongst stakeholders.** Building positive, trusting relationships with your employees, customers, and shareholders contributes to long-term sustainability—both for you personally and your company. Reflect for a moment on the number and scope of business interactions that occur on any given day. Trusting relationships improve efficiency and reduce the long-term cost of conflict, dishonesty, and disengagement. At HFE, promoting healthy relationships among leaders and employees allows all to perform at their highest level. The results at HFE and Popeyes indicate that healthy relationships do, in fact, lead to exceptional performance.

2. **Love aligns employees' personal values with their work values.** Generally, people desire to find meaning and purpose in their work and want the freedom to express their values in and through their work. As Joel explained, "When your personal values match your work values, you stand the best chance of being content. I have had offers to leave HFE but I have always said no because my personal and professional lives are in alignment, and that contentment is priceless."[31]

3. **A love-based culture increases its probability of profitability and sustainability.** Popeyes and HFE are models that demonstrate that love works. We shouldn't be so surprised. When we break the word *love* down to its actionable behaviors, we see it's a practical blueprint for human behavior. Love promotes and sustains the very attitudes and behaviors that benefit business.

We don't set out to create cultures of bad behavior; we allow bad behavior to infect our business culture, especially when under pressure. A culture that perseveres under pressure (maintains its core values) increases the odds of long-term sustainability because the principles of love provide a constancy of purpose that transcends interim shortfalls in results.

Further, love's actions protect individuals and, if governed properly, cultures from the self-serving behaviors that would otherwise destroy it. Why? Leaders and individuals rarely fail because of their competencies; they fail because of their character flaws. Clearly defined behavior expectations—across the board—limit our ability to fail.

The leadership principles of 1 Corinthians 13 build healthy relationships and strong companies. In *Love Works*, Joel Manby paraphrased seven leadership principles from 1 Corinthians 13:4–7: Love is Patient, Kind, Trusting, Unselfish, Truthful, Forgiving, and Dedicated. HFE has incorporated these principles into one of the organization's core values, *Serving Others: By being patient, kind, humble, respectful, selfless, forgiving, honest, and committed.*[32] Just as Joel did at HFE, these biblical principles can be put into practice in other diverse business settings—with a focus on expected behaviors, applied at all levels of an organization.

Realistically, though, many of us work for leaders who are ruled solely by the bottom line. If "love" is a command given to us individually, without regard to whom we work for, how can we implement its principles? Let's take a look at how we can personally apply these principles, regardless of our level in an organization.

First, reread 1 Corinthians 13:4–7, but dwell on it from a business perspective: "Love is patient, love is kind. It does not envy, it does not boast, it is not proud. It is not rude, it is not self-seeking, it is not easily angered, it keeps no record of wrongs. Love does not delight in evil but rejoices with the truth. It always protects, always trusts, always hopes, always perseveres."

What words came to mind? Patient, kind, generous, humble, respectful, selfless, forgiving, truthful, defend/guard, trustworthy, confident, committed . . . Don't each of these words have practical business applications, regardless of our roles in an organization?

Love . . .	Business Application
• Is patient	• Diligent
• Is kind	• Kind
• Does not envy	• Generous
• Does not boast	• Genuine
• Is not proud	• Humble
• Is not rude	• Respectful
• Is not self-seeking	• Selfless
• Is not easily angered	• Patient
• Keeps no record of wrongs	• Forgiving
• Rejoices with the truth	• Honest
• Protects	• Looks after
• Trusts	• Confident; trustworthy
• Hopes	• Courageous
• Perseveres	• Committed

Let's take this further. What does love look like in a business setting?

- Spending (sacrificing) time to help a business associate. Perhaps there's someone who needs your expertise, encouragement, generosity, or mentoring.
- Having the courage to be honest with a customer or coworker when you're wrong, apologizing and asking for forgiveness.
- Showing mercy to and forgiving another who made a mistake that cost you business.

- Respecting your competitors. Developing ground rules for fair play.
- Being quick to listen, slow to speak, and even slower to become angry.
- Leading with discretion by being careful with how you behave and speak in sensitive circumstances.
- Showing appreciation to someone who has helped or encouraged through a personal letter, e-mail, or one-on-one conversation.
- Sharing the truth with love, though it would be easier to avoid it.
- Holding yourself and others accountable for actions and behaviors; consider a small accountability group of trusted peers.
- Being humble to truth—listening to the advice or feedback of others with an open mind.
- Showing restraint and patience while dealing with a difficult employee or customer. As Joel Manby suggests, "Don't be patient with poor performance, be patient with how you respond to poor performance."[33]
- Having the courage to be clear. Clarify roles, responsibilities, and expectations between you and your stakeholders.
- Being consistent in who you say you are and what you promise, in all your business dealings.
- Rather than avoiding conflict, embracing it as an opportunity to honor God. Learn conflict resolution and mediation skills as a means to reconciling, healing, and restoring relationships damaged by turf wars, politics, and organizational conflict.
- Being responsible for every communication that leaves your mouth. Your words—verbal and written—have the power to destroy or heal. Reckless words harm. Complaining discourages others, lying is deceitful, gossip fuels conflict.

Conversely, a kind word of encouragement, wise counsel, and support makes another's life better. Communicating with love means understanding the power you have and using it wisely with care and discernment.

- Embracing adversity, uncertainty, and volatility as a means to trust God and encourage others going through similar challenges.
- Humbly acknowledging that God's redeeming love is at the heart of your success and significance as a leader at work and at home.
- Being generous with all you have and all you are.

History has been shaped by individual actions, actions that were the behavioral equivalent of love. Abraham Lincoln, George Washington, Martin Luther King, and William Wilberforce, among others, had the common trait of a steadfast love and perseverance in the face of opposition.

God gives us each the freedom to choose how we conduct our business and our life. Of the principles for success He's provided, the concept of love is among the strongest and most practical. Do you remember Charles Reade's powerful thought? "Sow an act and you reap a habit; sow a habit and you reap a character; sow a character and you reap a destiny." Our destiny is reaped based on each individual act we sow. Are you reaping a destiny based on love *or* the bottom line or love *and* the bottom line?

DISCUSSION GUIDE

1. Review the "Five Hidden Threats" and answer the questions. What threatens your business the most?
2. What insights from this chapter resonate most with you? Why?

3. Identify the pros and cons of leading with love in your business. Do the benefits outweigh the cost? Explain your response.

4. Review the love in action examples. What examples mean the most to you? Identify three actions you're willing to incorporate into your business.

5. What type of leader would you most like to work for? Describe the qualities of an ideal leader.

6. Are you that leader to someone today? Identify two actions you need to take in order to become the leader you aspire to be.

Notes

1. Joel Manby, *Love Works: Seven Timeless Principles for Effective Leaders* (Grand Rapids, MI: Zondervan, 2012), 24.
2. Manby, 18.
3. Manby, 19.
4. Manby, 20.
5. Manby, 20.
6. Manby, 23–24.
7. Manby, 29.
8. Manby, 22.
9. Manby, 32.
10. Manby, 33 and 34.
11. Manby, 34.
12. Manby, 61.
13. Manby, 66–67.
14. Manby, 62.
15. Manby, 64 and 66.
16. Manby, 97.
17. Manby, 98.
18. Manby, 99.
19. Manby, 112.
20. Manby, 122
21. Manby, 119–121, 122.
22. Manby, 122.
23. Patty Rasmussen, "Cheryl Bachelder Serves Chicken, Her Franchises and the World," April 9, 2013, *www.womenetics.com* (May 30, 2013).
24. Cheryl Bachelder, "Remembered and Remarkable," April 1, 2013, *www.thepurpose ofleadership.com.* (May 30, 2013).
25. Bachelder, *www.thepurposeofleadership.com.*
26. Manby, 23–24.
27. *www.merriam-webster.com*, "greed."

28. Mike Myatt, "10 Reasons Your Top Talent Will Leave You," December 13, 2012, *www.forbes.com* (May 21, 2013).
29. Myatt, *www.forbes.com*.
30. CPP Global Human Capital Report, "Workplace Conflict and How Businesses Can Harness it to Thrive." (Mountain View, CA: CPP, Inc., July 2008).
31. Manby, 180.
32. *www.hfecorp.com/commitment*, "Core Values & Mission" (May 30, 2013).
33. Manby, 50.

9

Priorities

From burning out to rekindling your spirit

Be joyful always; pray continuously; give thanks in all circumstances, for this is God's will for you in Christ Jesus.

—1 Thessalonians 5:16

Issue:

How do I deal with burnout in the workplace?

A significant issue is eating Mary up inside and ruining her and her family's lives: She's a workaholic, consumed by her job. She wakes up at 4:30 A.M. and is at work by 6:00 A.M. in order to get a good jump on the day. Around 7:30 P.M., she arrives home exhausted. She works almost a full day on Saturday and half a day on Sunday. On Sunday, she and her husband go to church, and then she comes home, works for a few hours, and does the weekly chores. On Monday morning, she wakes up and starts the cycle all over again. There's no break; one week slams into the next.

We talked about how Mary could find balance in her life. Mary broke into tears, saying, "I know I should find more balance, but my work demands keep piling up. I can never get caught up." After drying her tears, Mary promised, "Things are going to smooth out in a couple of months. When things get quiet, I'm going to talk to my boss about my schedule." I had already heard this story, several months ago. The demands Mary's employer placed on her were very real. It struck me, however, that she talked as if she had no choice in the matter. I thought, Who is responsible for this situation? Is it the company, who places unfair demands on an excellent employee, or is it the employee, who has accepted the circumstances, even at the expense of her health and her family?

Solution:

Keep the important things important.

In today's demanding, fast-paced world, it's easy to lose perspective on what's really important. We need to keep the important things important on a daily basis. Otherwise, we'll fall out of alignment with God's will and risk burnout.

Balancing one's personal and professional life is a serious and complex issue facing many people today. While one chapter of a book won't solve this issue, we'll gain insight by learning about two very busy leaders who are enjoying abundant life. We'll learn how their perspective and priorities allowed them to transcend the pressures of work. S. Truett Cathy, founder and chairman of Chick-fil-A, a nearly 1,000-unit restaurant chain, followed God's Fourth Commandment for rest, changing his life and impacting the thousands of employees who work for Chick-fil-A. Bob Naegele, former chairman and co-owner of Rollerblade, the company that turned in-line skating into an exercise phenomenon, demonstrates how appreciation for God's blessings translated to showing his appreciation to Rollerblade's employees. In both cases, these leaders kept perspective on what was most important and, as a result, enjoyed a harvest of love, peace, and joy.

S. TRUETT CATHY
"Keeping the Important Things Important"

S. Truett Cathy is no stranger to hard work. He also understands the challenges of finding time to rest. More than fifty years ago, Truett and his brother, Ben, opened a small restaurant called the Dwarf Grill in an Atlanta suburb. In 1946, when their first week of business had ended, Ben and Truett sat down, exhausted after the Saturday dinner crowd had all but left. Between the two of them, the brothers had covered six consecutive twenty-four-hour shifts. "What do you think, Truett?" Ben asked. "I think we ought to close tomorrow," Truett replied. From the very beginning, the Cathy brothers told their customers, "We're open twenty-four hours a day, but not on Sunday."[1]

"Closing on Sunday has become a distinctive principle of my Christian background," says Truett. "From my infancy, my Sunday School teachers and pastors stressed that Sunday is the Lord's day. I see another reason. God told the Israelites to work only six days so the seventh day could be used for rest. Our bodies and minds need time off to recharge. Lastly, while I was growing up, Sunday was an important day for family times together. For the last fifty-four years, I've accepted that as a principle and have honored God by doing it. God has honored us and the business because of it."[2]

The results speak for themselves. On Sunday, you'll find Truett doing the two things he loves most: teaching Sunday School to teens (which he has done for the past forty-five years) and being with his family. On the professional front, that single restaurant in 1946 became the cornerstone of Chick-fil-A, now a nearly 1,000-unit restaurant chain.

Truett made the we're-not-open-on-Sunday decision in 1946 and has remained committed to the principle ever since. As a result, neither Truett nor any of Chick-fil-A's 40,000 restaurant employees work on Sunday. The traditional business world has called this decision crazy because Chick-fil-A potentially passes on 15 to 20 percent of its possible sales. Truett, Chick-fil-A's founder and chairman, sees it in an entirely different way. "I believe God gave His laws not to make life harder, but to make it better," he explains. "This is the formula God has given us for success. In this case it's definitely easier to succeed than to work seven days a week and miss the blessing."

S. Truett Cathy lives his life on a simple principle: Keep the important things in life important. He tells people that success is not defined in only one area of life but in several. "We have to ask ourselves what's really important," he says. "I have seen people who were very successful in business but a total flop in relationships with their family and the other important things in life. I have seen many fathers who loved their children and were anxious to give them the material things they never had as a child, but failed to give them what's really important. For me, the most important thing is my relationship with the Lord and to live my life as a role model for my children. It's nice to have the material things that go with what people generally classify as 'business success'—the nice home and nice cars. All that is secondary when it comes to my family."

I met Truett at Chick-fil-A headquarters in Atlanta a number of years ago. I imagined that I was going to meet the very busy chairman and founder of a fast-food business that grossed almost $800,000,000 in sales the previous year (in 2012 the company had sales of $4.6 billion). Instead, the person I met could have been my grandfather. Entering the grounds, I felt a sense of peace and serenity as I drove along a winding road through seventy-three acres of beautifully landscaped woods and ponds. After parking my car, I walked up to the main entrance and spotted Chick-fil-A's corporate purpose statement. It read:

> To glorify God by being a faithful steward
> of all that is entrusted to us.
> To have a positive influence on all
> who come in contact with Chick-fil-A.

I entered and announced my appointment to the receptionist. Quickly, Truett's assistant greeted me with, "I apologize. Mr. Cathy is running about twenty minutes late at lunch with two important visitors. Why not have some lunch in our restaurant while you wait?"

When I met Truett, he was saying goodbye to his important visitors: two thirteen-year-old boys who wanted to see Chick-fil-A's operations. In addition to his natural family of three children, twelve grandchildren, and eleven great-grandchildren (as of February 2012), Truett is grandpa to more than 150 "foster grandchildren" through WinShape Homes, a foster care program established by Truett and his wife Jeannette in 1987.

Talking with Truett about business and leadership, I could see where his passion lies: in his faith in God; his family; the corporate staff; and the 40,000 restaurant employees, the majority of whom are young people whom he considers family. As we finished, Truett gave me a tour of his automobile museum and walked me to the entrance of the headquarters. Summer in Atlanta can be hot, and this day was no exception. As we stood in the parking lot, Truett turned to me and said, "Get in. I'll give you a lift to your car."

"Is this your car?" I asked as we looked at an old, beat-up Toyota pickup. Truett responded, "Nah, I got it for one of my boys who's heading to college. I got it and fixed it up so he could have it to get around. I need to test-drive it to make sure everything is okay."

As we passed the bronze plaque with the corporate purpose statement, I reread the first statement: "To glorify God by being a faithful steward of all that is entrusted to us." *Wow, I bet they get some flak for that*, I thought. As if he could hear my thoughts, Truett explained, "Our executive staff initially came up with that statement at a retreat in North Georgia. We were going through tough times back in 1982, and we had an urgency to solve some serious business issues. During a long discussion, my son Dan spoke up. 'Why are we in business?' he asked. 'Why are we here? Why are we alive?' At first, I considered these to be simple questions. 'Why are we wasting time talking about 'why' when we need to talk about how we are going to get past this crisis?' Instead of brushing these questions aside, however, I stopped and said, 'Maybe we do need to answer these questions.'"

Truett went on to explain that they eventually came up with the corporate purpose statement, to provide clarity on what they believed was most important. In 1983, his staff made a plaque of the corporate purpose statement and gave it to him as a Christmas gift. "I was honored," he recalls. "That statement summarizes my attitude better than anything else. I have always wanted to influence the people in our organization, not by pressing anything on them, but by my attitude, my lifestyle."

As I drove up the interstate to catch a flight back home, I reflected on my visit. I realized that Truett lived up to that corporate purpose statement. He honored God by being a good steward, and he certainly had a positive influence on me. Despite the business demands and pressures placed on the chairman of a 1,000-unit restaurant chain, this grandpa was living his life with the conviction of what was most important to him.

Understanding Truett's priorities in life clarifies his decision to close all his restaurants on Sunday. Sunday is traditionally the third most active day for restaurant sales, generating approximately 14 percent of the weekly and annual business. Roughly

$50 billion will be spent in restaurants on Sundays, and none of it will be spent in a Chick-fil-A. Not only does this translate into lost revenue potential, but it also means Truett has to deal with the considerable pressure that comes from mall developers around the country. They want Chick-fil-A to be open in order to feed their customers.

In his autobiography, *It's Easier to Succeed Than to Fail*, Truett recalls the time he received a letter from a developer whose mall is among the largest in the United States. This letter was received at a time of increased competition and declining sales. While polite, the letter pressured Truett to open the mall's Chick-fil-A on Sundays. It included many valid reasons.

The letter closed by explaining: "We have thousands of employees and Sunday strollers who are being denied the right to eat at your place on Sunday afternoon. If you feel that the points we set forth in this letter are valid, and you will consider keeping Chick-fil-A open on Sunday, we would like to offer our contribution in the amount of $5,000 to the churches or organizations of your choice."

Truett responded, explaining in detail his decision. Truett's letter closed with, "Your thoughts are well-received. You are just the kind of person we would like to honor with any reasonable request, but please understand, we cannot compromise on certain principles."[3]

While Truett has had considerable external pressure from the business world, he has never felt any internal pressure to give in. He knows what's important. "You can't be a people pleaser to everyone," he expounds. "Even the people who disagree with you will respect you for your convictions. Besides, how can I teach the boys in my Sunday School class to observe the Lord's day if cash registers are jingling in my restaurants?"[4]

The principles that drive Truett's personal and professional life take precedence over the pressures of business. Rather than reacting to business's carrots (rewards) and sticks (business demands), he responds to the prescription God has laid out for him. This frees him from the shackles business demands place on him.

I came to Truett looking for answers to the complex issue of work and family balance. What I found was a man who didn't even see it as an issue. He was simply living the life God intended him to live and keeping the important things important.

ROBERT O. NAEGELE JR.
"Appreciating What's Important"

Meeting with Bob Naegele in his downtown Minneapolis office on a sunny October afternoon, I observed a man having fun. Immediately, I sensed the enthusiasm and joy in his demeanor. I found his enthusiasm odd, considering Bob was waiting to see if his proposal to buy the Minnesota Twins baseball team was going to be accepted. Considering the magnitude of the opportunity, I assumed Bob would be stressed and distracted. That wasn't the case. Bob's circumstances didn't matter; he was enjoying life regardless of them.

It wasn't always that way for Bob. Like most people, he's had his share of challenging times. "My life has been a series of wrecks and rescues," explains Bob. Today, however, he no longer lives in fear; he lives in appreciation. He appreciates what life has given him because he knows it's all a gift from God.

"Fear used to be a big part of my life," Bob says. "I had a deep-seated fear that I was going to come up short. As a child and into adulthood, I feared death. Fear also played a role in my business life. Fear was a motivator. Fear told me to get the job done, or it would cost me my job. Its total motivation is self-preservation. I have had my ups and downs in life, but looking back, every time there was a wreck, there was a rescue."

He is quick to tell of his personal encounter with Jesus Christ, one that altered the direction of his life, his family's life, and the lives of friends, employees, and business associates. "Through Him, I discovered that God loved me so much that He had sent His son to die for me. I had never known about that love. In addition, I found that God was profoundly interested in me, personally and professionally, and wanted me to succeed in every area of my life. God came to my rescue. On a professional basis, I became a more caring leader. At home, I became a better husband and father. I learned to focus on the important things like trust, respect, and honoring my wife, and they made a huge difference. It was amazing to see the positive impact in our marriage."

Bob's career has spanned close to fifty years, half of which was in the outdoor advertising industry. The period between 1985 and 1995 proved to be the most eventful. Bob and fifteen others transformed an unknown inline skate into Rollerblade, a company that created a new way for millions of people to have fun and get exercise.

Bob and his team had their share of challenges at Rollerblade. "My experience at Rollerblade reflected my life: ups and downs and a wreck that needed a rescue," Bob relates. They struggled for years trying to get recognized. Even though they had a great product, no one knew about it. The company was struggling financially and didn't have the resources to market its product the way it needed to be marketed.

Bob recalls, "I remember one particular night when I was growing fearful and anxious about whether we were going to make it. I remember reading Philippians 4:6, 'Do not be anxious about anything, but in everything, by prayer and petition, with thanksgiving, present your requests to God.' I cried out, 'God, please help us . . . nobody knows about Rollerblade.'"

Two weeks later, the Minnesota Vikings were playing the Chicago Bears on *Monday Night Football*. During the week of the game, on national television, Mike Ditka, head coach of the Chicago Bears, commented, "We're playing the Vikings at that 'Rollerdome' up in Minneapolis." Rollerblade's marketing people jumped on it, and "Rollerblade" became a household word and an overnight success.

The Rollerdome incident helped Bob remember who was really in charge. Today, the incident helps him appreciate how good God has been to him. It also gives him a tremendous appreciation for the others around him who have contributed to Rollerblade's success.

Upon selling his 50 percent share of Rollerblade to Nordica, an Italian ski boot manufacturer, Bob wanted to show his appreciation to Rollerblade's employees. "My father used to say, 'Gratitude unspoken is ingratitude.' So, how do you show gratitude? By saying 'thank you' in a meaningful way."

Rollerblade employee Ann, six months pregnant, called her husband, sobbing. Immediately assuming the worst, his reaction turned to joy as Ann described the note of gratitude and the $11,000 check she received from Bob Naegele and his wife Ellis. Ann wasn't the only employee to receive a generous gift of thanks from the Naegeles. All 280 employees of Rollerblade received financial gifts, totaling in excess of $4 million. Every employee, from warehouse worker to department manager, received a check based on years of service with the company.[5]

"Ellis and I knew we wanted to do something," says Bob. "We knew our motivation, but we didn't quite know how to go about doing it. We had questions like, 'How do we give the gift?' 'Who should receive the gift?' 'How do we do this fairly?' With our motivation in place, we sought God's guidance on the how and the who. That's the great thing about having a relationship with God. When you are in God's will, things seem to move along. Everything came together smoothly. There wasn't a great deal of guesswork and accountant's projections involved."

The timing of the Rollerblade sale and the details coincided perfectly with the Christmas season. Bob's stock was sold in November 1995, and the details of their gift-giving plan were in place the week before Christmas. "Everything came together at a time that was so meaningful to Ellis and me, a time when you expect the miracles of Christmas to happen. We coordinated with Rollerblade's Vice President of Human Relations what we wanted to do. A list of all the employees was composed, and Ellis and I sat down at our kitchen table and started to write the checks. Waves of joy would overcome us as we saw each person's face in our minds, wrote a note of thanks, and signed the check."

The gifts were mailed the week before Christmas, and began to arrive at employees' homes on December 21. The joy spread rapidly. Rollerblade spokesperson Deborah Autrey said, "It was a complete surprise that came out of the blue. People were laughing and crying, hugging. I have never seen people in such a stupor." When the good news reached Matt, the director of product marketing, he immediately phoned his wife and asked her to open the mail. When she did, Matt heard sobs. He had been with the company eleven years, making his check an estimated $21,120. "It was very moving. It was very heartfelt for us. We were extremely shocked and extremely grateful for his generosity."[6]

As I interviewed Bob, the meaning of the biblical term "cheerful giver" became clear. Joy was part of who he was. During our interview, Bob used the word *joy* fifteen times, repeatedly speaking of the waves of joy created by giving. "Joy is infectious; it's explosive; you can't repress it," he explains. "We tried to slip the rock into the pond by being quiet about our gift to the employees. What we found was that giving motivated by God creates a ripple effect that creates significant waves of joy."

The first wave of joy Bob described was when he and Ellis wrote out the checks from their kitchen table. "Ellis and I received our second wave of joy when the thank you letters started to arrive at our home," says Bob. "Letter after letter after letter, it was wonderful! It would happen almost every day for months. One young couple described how they put a down payment on their first house; one couple wrote that they put the money into a fund for their child's education; one guy and his wife sent us a picture of the house they just bought. It was a financial impact, a material impact, but more importantly, it had a spiritual impact."

Here are some of those notes:

"I want to thank you from the bottom of my student loans for remembering even an intern at Rollerblade. I was completely shocked, stunned, and overjoyed all at the same time."

Mindy

"In order to express our heartfelt thanks for your gift, we have made a donation to our church's building fund debt. We have a lot to be thankful for."

Jay and Kathy

"Your gift was incredibly generous and has been placed in our son's name for his education. One day, I will be able to tell Carson about my life with Rollerblade and specifically you and your family. I cannot really explain or describe our appreciation in this card; words don't seem enough. You have touched my life in more ways than you can imagine. I thank you now and one day I would like Carson to thank you in person."

John and Jane

"Your gift has been a source of encouragement. Not only has it been financially uplifting but it has sent a powerful spiritual message. Your gift will never be forgotten. May God bless you always."

Bill and Angela

The third wave of joy came from an unlikely source—the media. Bob's original intent was to keep this gift a private matter, but it didn't take long before the media heard about the generous gifts.

Bob recalls receiving a phone call from one of his managers, Matt. "Matt called me and said 'Bob, the press is going to find out. What should we do?' My initial reaction was to keep this story quiet. Then I said, 'Fine, it's a great opportunity to give God the glory.'"

The media communicated a wonderful message. Headlines across the country included "Gifts to Workers Set Naegele Apart," "Gracious Thank You Bonus Bucks Current Business Trend," and "Sharing the Wealth—A Good Deed Sets a Good Example." As news spread, so did the letters from all over the country. The message of giving touched a wide range of people. A teacher wrote,

> After teaching for 31 years in Wayzata Public Schools, I have yet to receive more than an apple on American Education Day. I congratulate you for giving part of your profits back to your employees.
>
> *Larry*

U.S. Senator Byron Dorgan of North Dakota was so moved he decided to make a presentation on the floor of the U.S. Senate: "Mr. President, I would like to talk just briefly about two Americans I want to bring to the attention of my colleagues—two heroes of mine. I have never met these men. I talked with one of them on the phone the other day, a fellow named Bob Naegele. I learned about Mr. Naegele and his company in an article I read in the *Star Tribune* when I was traveling through Minneapolis the other day by plane." (He then told the story.) "What this man was saying to them was: You mattered. You people who worked in the plant and factories and helped make this product, you are the ones who made me successful. You made me some money, and I want to share it with you. What a remarkable story. What a hero! It seems to me if more CEOs in this country would understand what Mr. Naegele understands, this country would be a better place."

Joy is a term that can be misunderstood; sometimes made synonymous with happiness or exhilaration. It's so easy to focus on the benevolence of the person, rather than the source of their inspiration. Bob explains, "I used to be stressed out and fearful, not knowing what my future holds, but now I know who holds my future."

Bob defines the joy he lives and speaks like this: "Joy is an inner feeling provided by God, while exhilaration is the thrill of the moment. That's what business people seek—the thrill of the moment, the thrill of the accomplishment, the landing of the deal. That's why business is so attractive to people. It's also why business people burn out. They're always trying to reach for something more without fully appreciating what they have. But exhilaration is a short-term fix driven by circumstance. Joy is much deeper than exhilaration. Joy comes from being motivated by God to do things that matter, that give Him the glory."

CONCLUSION

I was in downtown Minneapolis, racing between appointments. While typically calm and collected, I was in a foul mood. I had just left a frustrating meeting and had thirty minutes to get to my next appointment. Pristine snow-covered streets had turned wet and muddy. Watching my shoes get muddier made me more aggravated because I wanted to look good for my next appointment. Knowing that two shoeshine stands were located on the way to my next appointment, I quickly ran to the stand I preferred. It was convenient, provided fast service, and was directly on my route. There was a wait, so I decided to head to the other stand, about a block away.

Thankfully, the second stand had no line. The shoeshine man sat in the big, comfortable chair eating his sandwich. As I raced up to the stand, the elderly man rose slowly to greet me. Neatly dressed in dark blue slacks and a navy shirt, the shirt's emblem proudly displayed his name, Jake. Smiling, he glanced at my muddy shoes and said, "Man, you came to the right place. Hop up and let Jake take care of you."

Jumping into the chair, I began fuming as I recalled the meeting I had just left. I thought about my presentation, given to ten surgeons from a prestigious medical practice. I had volunteered my services to help these physicians understand the importance of showing respect for their patients. This was a personally significant opportunity, as a member of this clinic had performed my recent back surgery. I felt I had been treated as a spine, not a person, and hoped to show them how to be more respectful of the patient and how to treat patients as customers.

The meeting was a disaster. The surgeons became indignant, claiming, "We can't afford to do that! Do you know what kind of pressure we're under? Time is money and our caseload is already overloaded. We don't have time to hand-hold every patient."

I had been working long hours under considerable pressure trying to grow my new business. Recalling the details of the meeting set off a chain reaction of negative thoughts: I get no appreciation for my efforts. I'm behind in my work. I probably have to work late to prepare for my presentation tomorrow. I'm tired. This day stinks! I caught myself going through my complaint list and snapped out of it.

I glanced at Jake as he meticulously cleaned my shoes and made sure he had wiped away any trace of mud. I watched as he wrapped an old cloth tightly around two fingers and dipped them into black shoe polish. Using slow circular motions, he rubbed the polish deep into my shoes. I was mesmerized by the meticulous detail he used to shine my shoes. Each stroke began to transform my cold and tired feet into a comfortable and warm respite from the day. I found myself starting to relax.

Without looking up, Jake said, "Life sure is good, ain't it?" I sarcastically replied, "That depends on your perspective." Jake looked up and said, "I don't know about you, but the good Lord has blessed me with a great ninety years." I asked, "What's the key to your success?" He smiled and said, "Appreciation. I appreciate everything the Lord has given me." Jake went on to describe a life of poverty, struggles, and hard times, yet his stories were filled with many blessings, including a job he loved and a loving family.

His comments stopped me. I thought about my meeting with the surgeons. They were upset about their time pressures, and they were clearly not at peace. Financially, they had everything they needed, yet they were stressed and complaining about their circumstances. I thought, These surgeons have a lot to be thankful for, yet don't appreciate what they have. On the other hand, Jake has lived a tough life, has very little in the way of material possessions, but is truly filled with peace and joy.

A seven-minute shoeshine transformed a bad day into a good day. My circumstances hadn't changed, but my perspective had. For the first time, I understood what it meant to be joyful always and to give thanks in all circumstances. Quite frankly, I had never been able to put my arms around the concept of "being joyful always." I thought, How can I be joyful when I am under such stress and feel so lousy? It was even more of a stretch when it came to "giving thanks in all circumstances." I believed that it was one thing to muster up some joy, but to actually give thanks in *all* circumstances? Even the bad ones? That's a stretch! Jake helped me gain perspective on what's important. He helped me see how God wastes nothing; He uses all circumstances for the good of those who love Him.

Truett, Bob, and Jake help us understand how it's possible to be joyful regardless of circumstances, financial pressure, and time pressure. We all face times when we're overworked and overwhelmed. For many, this is a temporary condition that improves over time. For others, the situation continues and results in burn-out and hopelessness. Whether we're just having a bad day or are dealing with a serious case of hopelessness, don't despair. We can rekindle the spirit that lies within us regardless of our present circumstances.

Despite the differences in their backgrounds, Truett, Bob, and Jake had some amazing similarities.

- As Thoreau once said, they hear the beat of "a different drummer." They lived their lives as an expression of living within the will of God. They didn't define their happiness by the world's standards, but by the will of God. They dictated their pace rather than having the pace dictated for them.
- Although never intending to do so, their decisions made public statements that impacted others. Truett's decision to keep his restaurants closed on Sundays was a statement to his employees regarding the importance of rest and family time. Bob's gifts to the employees of Rollerblade said, "You matter, and I appreciate what you do." Jake's statement, "I'm thankful in all circumstances," has had a significant impact on me and probably many others who thought they just needed a shoeshine.
- They maintained perspective. They kept the important things important and put circumstances in their proper perspective.
- Each man made a very simple decision in the midst of a complex world. Truett's decision to close his stores could have become complex as he thought through the lost income and strained mall developer relationships, but for him the decision was simple. He was just following God's instructions for success. Bob's decision to reward his employees was fraught with legal and accounting details, yet his desire to show appreciation was heartfelt and simple. He knew the complexities of his decision would work themselves out.

Jake could have complained about the things he never had, yet he chose to appreciate and make the best of what he did receive.

Have you ever met someone and felt certain negative or positive vibes? Have you ever felt tense when someone else was tense or felt at ease because someone else was at ease? From these men, I felt love, peace, and joy. These were the byproducts of living lives of faith in the midst of a complex world. They each had abundant life and an overflowing spirit. I left each meeting feeling energized, loved, and inspired.

When we're burned out, we drain others. When we have an overflowing spirit, we inspire and energize others. Don't take burnout lightly. Perhaps a simple analogy will help us move in the right direction. Sometimes, we, like a car, have trouble getting going.

Diagnostic Step: Check whether the following symptoms exist:

- My battery needs charging. (I have difficulty getting started in the morning.)
- My idle is set too high. (The pace of my life is too hectic.)
- I left the lights on overnight. (I don't stop thinking about work when I go to bed.)
- I'm riding rough and need a tune-up. (I'm not as effective at work as I would like to be.)

Repair Step 1: Charge the battery.

God is the source of my power and strength. Pray, give thanks, and gain perspective. One simple exercise is to count your blessings (literally). When you're feeling particularly stressed, take a moment and rattle off a list of the things you're thankful for.

Repair Step 2: Set the idle at the right speed.

Live the pace that's right for you, not the world's pace. Make the important things important and simplify your life by cutting back unnecessary externals.

Repair Step 3: Turn off your lights each night.

Put closure on each day. Create time to rest daily and weekly and make sure a good night's sleep separates each day.

Repair Step 4: Get a tune-up.

Create a daily rejuvenation plan for the mind, body, and soul. Make sure each day has a morning, afternoon, and evening break.

Repair Step 5: Take a ride in the country.

Sometimes all we need is a change of scenery. It could be that a small break or vacation will do the trick. Sometimes, we may need to change our environment. If you performed steps 1 through 5, and you still find your energy drained, you may need to find another environment, one that will rejuvenate your soul.

DISCUSSION GUIDE

1. What causes you to burn out from your job? What, specifically, is the root cause?
2. How's your perspective? Are you satisfied or dissatisfied with your present situation? Why?
3. Are your actions in alignment with the things that are most important to you?
4. What changes could you make to keep the important things important?
5. What can you do to rejuvenate your spirit daily?

Notes

1. S. Truett Cathy, *It's Easier to Succeed Than to Fail* (Nashville: Oliver-Nelson Books, 1989), 69.
2. Ibid., 70.
3. Ibid., 75.
4. Ibid., 70.
5. "Rollerblade employees rewarded for service," *Naples Daily News*, January 7, 1996.
6. Ibid.

10

Redemption

From slavery to freedom

For it is by grace you have been saved, through faith—and this not from yourselves, it is the gift of God.

—Ephesians 2:8

Issue:

How do I recover from a personal or professional failure?

"**M**ike, this is an intervention."

Mike was stunned to the very core. At twenty-five years old, he had the world by the tail. He was a few months into a promising new job and was to be married in just three weeks.

But before that day was over, he had his first glimpse of what would come to be an important way to describe who he was.

Hi, my name's Mike and I'm an alcoholic.

Mike isn't alone. Some of my other friends have been struggling to recover from past failures, too. Tom is a talented, driven, and successful CEO who doesn't see the role he played in either a painful divorce or emotionally distant kids. He remains headstrong and set in his ways; he's just not open to the changes he must make to overcome his flaws. Jeff, on the other hand, lost his job when his company downsized. He's lost hope and given up. At fifty-five years old, with tremendous talent, skills, and experience, he's bought into the hype that the baby boomer generation is irrelevant in today's new economy.

In each of these situations, pride is the root of the issue. The Greek translation of pride is "blindness" and "self-centeredness." Whether due to pride, denial, or fear, we can be blind to the personal transformation needed in order to improve our lives and the lives around us.

Solution:

Trust in the God of second chances.

Personal redemption and transformation isn't a program, nor is it a personal growth plan. Redemption is a gift of God. Through this gift, our failings can be transformed into new beginnings, resulting in lives of success and significance. Jesus' purpose was to give us life, regardless of our past imperfections.

In this chapter, we'll get to know two leaders who fell hard, but through the grace of a loving God found new life overflowing with meaning and purpose. Mark Whitacre and Mike Sime both made bad choices, over and over again. They were blind to their weaknesses. In the end, like each of us, the only way they could change was through God Himself. The result was two individuals whose lives were radically transformed.

MARK WHITACRE
"From Enslaved to Redeemed"

It was a warm August morning in Chapel Hill, North Carolina. Mark Whitacre had made what appeared to be the last of a series of bad decisions. He entered his garage, turned on his car, and, clutching a photo of his family, waited for the fumes to end his nightmare. "I didn't want to live and doubted that I deserved to. My selfishness and pride had robbed my family of the stability and security a father should provide." How did a bright and gifted business executive fall so far from grace so quickly?

"I started at Archer Daniels Midland (ADM) in 1989 when I was thirty-two, as president of the bio-products division," Mark explains. "At that time, ADM was the fifty-sixth largest company on the Fortune 500 and one of the largest food additive companies in the world, with over $70 billion in revenue and 30,000 employees. ADM's ingredients are in the foods people eat and drink every day: Kellogg's cereals, Kraft Foods, Tyson Foods, Coca-Cola, and Pepsi.

"Within three years I was promoted to corporate vice president and corporate officer. The industry analysts at *Fortune* magazine stated I was likely to become the next COO and president of ADM when the then-seventy-year-old president retired. My total compensation was seven figures, my beautiful wife, loving family, and I lived in a mansion, and I had free access to corporate jets."

By 1992, greed and pride were changing him. "Work consumed me. I was greedy. No matter how much I earned, it was never enough." Mark's wife, Ginger, noticed the changes.

"In November 1992, Ginger started digging deeper into our conversations. She was direct. What was going on at work? Why was I so intense? Why did I seem so unhappy? So I finally told her.

The top executives of ADM, including myself, were conducting an illegal, international price-fixing scheme. I explained how we were getting together with our competitors and fixing the prices of several key ingredients. We had basically formed an international cartel. We were stealing a billion dollars a year from our large food and beverage customers, and that increased cost was being passed on to consumers. Basically, we were stealing from everyone around the world who bought groceries.

"Ginger didn't like what she heard and said I should turn myself in to the FBI. I told her I could go to prison and that we would lose our home, our cars, and our lifestyle. She persisted, 'Either turn yourself in to the FBI, or I will do it for you!' And she meant it!

"An hour later I was confessing to an FBI agent about my white-collar crime. In the process, I became an informant with the distinction of being the highest-level Fortune 500 executive ever to be a whistleblower. In reality, it was Ginger who was the true whistleblower. If not for a thirty-four-year-old stay-at-home mom of three young children, the largest price-fixing scandal in U.S. history might never have been exposed.

"After confessing my role in the scheme, I agreed to work undercover for the FBI. Working undercover was an extremely stressful life—a life at odds with itself. For example, I acted like a loyal executive, building the company during the day, and tearing it down during the evenings. At 6 A.M., I would meet the FBI, who would shave my chest in order to tape mini-microphones to it. They would check the batteries of the tape recorders in my briefcase and in a special notebook. During the day, I recorded my peers. From 6 P.M. to midnight, I met with the FBI to turn over the tapes and endure what seemed to be endless debriefings.

"The price-fixing meetings weren't held just in ADM's headquarters in Decatur, Illinois. They were conducted all around the world—Paris, Mexico City, Vancouver, Hong Kong, and Zurich, to name a few cities—and I recorded them all with three audio devices.

"After two years of wearing the wire, I was spent. I didn't know if I worked for the FBI or ADM. I began to spiral out of control, like a nervous breakdown. Once, during a horrific thunderstorm, I took a leaf blower to our driveway at 3 A.M., trying to clear the leaves to keep up appearances. I was still wearing my shirt and tie. Ginger heard the noise from the bedroom window and came out to the driveway under an umbrella.

"Although I hadn't been there for Ginger, she had a strength to draw on—her faith. Her personal relationship with Christ had sustained her since she was thirteen. In contrast, I went to church, but I was just going through the motions. If someone had asked me if I was a Christian, I would have said, 'Yes, I go to church almost every Sunday.'

"Ginger yelled to me, 'You need to come back into the house. You need to come back to your family. More than anything, you need to have God in your life.'

"'Who needs God?' I retorted. 'I'm going to be the next president of the fifty-sixth largest company in America.'

"She looked as angry as I've ever seen her. 'I'm proud of what you're doing,' she said, 'that you're working with the FBI, but you are *not* going to be president of ADM. You need to get that through your mind. You're bringing the top three executives down; they're likely to go to jail. You'll be fired once they learn what you've done.'

"She left me in the driveway, and I knew she was right. I wouldn't be able to stay at ADM. I couldn't imagine living without my position and income. It was as though I was addicted to success. I was obsessed with material things. I began to think how I was going to protect myself.

"I concluded that I could steal what would have been my severance pay—$9.5 million. How could ADM prosecute me for stealing millions when they were stealing billions? I felt immune. So I submitted several bogus invoices to ADM from companies that I owned, until ADM had paid me $9.5 million.

"In return for wearing a wire, I received full immunity from any criminal case—as long as I didn't break any other laws. In June 1995, ADM learned I was the informant. They immediately contacted the FBI and notified them that I was no white knight. I had stolen $9.5 million. The gig was up. I lost the immunity agreement.

"The four agents with whom I worked for almost three years had every reason to reject me, but amazingly, they still supported me. They helped me obtain an excellent lawyer. They worked behind the scenes with the prosecutors to help me get a plea deal.

"The prosecutors heard the arguments of the FBI agents and my lawyer, and they agreed to a three-year plea deal. But there was more. As part of the plea deal, the FBI agents would be able to present the same arguments to the sentencing judge that had been presented to the prosecutors. My lawyer felt that I would get a six-month prison sentence. He called Ginger and me to his Chicago office to review the details of 'the deal of a lifetime.' There, I proved I was still my own worst enemy. I rejected the deal and fired my attorney.

"I hired new attorneys and started preparing for trial. One year later, I received a ten-and-a-half year prison sentence.

"I could have taken my Chicago attorney's counsel in humility. I should have been broken at that point. The decisions that I made—isolated in my own mind—were coming back to haunt me. How would I survive a decade in prison? How would my family survive? I was losing all hope."

Emotionally and spiritually bankrupt, Mark's thoughts and choices brought him to the point of suicide that morning, August 9, 1997. His mind was tortured by a future that seemed hopeless: How will my marriage survive? How will I ever provide for my family? How could a convicted felon ever get a job? How would the four FBI agents ever forgive me? In complete hopelessness, Mark drifted into unconsciousness as carbon monoxide fumes took the place of oxygen.

On that morning, the Whitacre's groundskeeper came to work . . . two hours earlier than expected, and saved Mark's life. Despite God's intervention in his life, Mark was completely depressed as he looked at the living hell his life had become. He prayed, "God, if you want to keep me alive, show me your purpose!"

"About a month later, I was befriended by Ian Howes, a CFO in the biotech industry, who had read about my case and my suicide attempt. Ian showed genuine interest in me as a person and listened without condemning. There was something different about this man, which I had not seen in other friendships.

"He was there when all of my other friends had deserted me. Ian was part of a businessmen's group, Christian Business Men's Connection (CBMC). As we got together, we read the Bible and used a study called *Operation Timothy*. He caused me to consider the claims of Christ. Who was He? What did He do? What difference does it make? Ian gave me my first glimmer of hope in that desperate time. He spent time with me each week planting seeds of the Gospel that would ultimately lead me to Christ.

"On March 4, 1998, I entered federal prison in Springfield, Missouri, as inmate number 07543-424. Shortly thereafter, I was transferred to the prison in Yazoo, Mississippi. In Yazoo, Chuck Colson, President Nixon's 'hatchet man' and founder of Prison Fellowship, came to visit me. Chuck became one of my mentors, sharing the same truths from the Bible that Ian had taught me. He said God loved me and no matter what mistakes I had made, God could forgive me.

"For the first time, I understood being a Christian was not about going to church every Sunday or what I did or didn't do; it was about a relationship with God. In a prison cell in June 1998, I got on my knees, asked God to forgive me, and surrendered to Christ. At last, I had peace.

"It was the first time I felt peace in my entire forty-one years of life. I didn't know my purpose. I had no idea what lay ahead. I just felt strongly that God would take care of my family."

In the weeks that followed, Mark continued to worry about his burdens—particularly about how his family would survive financially. The one difference was that now he was talking candidly to God about his fears.

"I was only three months into a decade-long prison sentence, but for the first time in my life, I was content. My life's void, which I had tried to fill with money, mansions, cars, and business success, was now satisfied. Before entering prison, I thought prison would be the end of my life, only to find that it was the beginning.

"I actually found my life more fulfilled in prison, making $20 a month, than it was when I received a seven-figure salary. I would wake up every morning really excited, praying 'Lord, lead me to the person I can help today.' Boy, did he ever deliver! Every single day there was a new assignment to help . . . help an inmate learn to read, help another get his GED, help another write a letter to a loved one. Looking back, my time in prison was very productive and fulfilling."

Just two months after surrendering the burden of his family's financial survival to God, an attorney contacted Ginger. "He informed her that companies including Tyson Foods, Pepsi, Coca-Cola, and Kraft, who had won hundreds of millions of dollars in class action suits against ADM, wanted to assist our family while I was in prison. They set up a trust fund that allowed Ginger to go back to college to finish her degree. She became an elementary school teacher and was the 2007 Teacher of the Year in Pensacola, Florida. The trust fund also assisted with our children's college educations, house payments, and other bills." As Mark exclaimed, "That's an amazing miracle! The victims of the fraud case assisted the perpetrator's family!"

Mark was also concerned about how to maintain his relationship with his family, and with good reason. Statistics indicate that 99 percent of people incarcerated five years or longer get divorced. "Over the course of my sentence, I was relocated three times, and each time my wife and children moved near the prison and visited me. The visiting hours in federal prison camps are from 5 to 8 P.M. on Friday evenings and 8 A.M. to 3 P.M. on Saturdays and Sundays. Basically seventeen hours per weekend. My family came every Friday, Saturday, Sunday, and holiday for nine years. I got to know my kids better in prison than when I was living at home. It's a miracle that I'm still married and have a good relationship with my children.

"At 8 A.M. on December 21, 2006, I was released from prison as a forty-nine-year-old convicted felon. The following day, I was hired by Paul Willis, CEO of Cypress Systems, Inc., into the same industry I had left."

Today, Mark lives a full and very active life of purpose. Beyond his full-time job as COO and chief science officer of Cypress Systems, Inc., Mark speaks all over the world sharing his story of redemption, giving people going through adversity hope in a loving God. He also has an active prison ministry, getting people ready for prison and helping them transition back to life as they leave prison. Mark's story was documented in a bestselling book, *The Informant*, and also inspired a movie by the same name, which starred Matt Damon as Mark.

Mark was living the best life this world has to offer, and he now understands that it wasn't life. "On that day in my prison cell when I asked for forgiveness and accepted Jesus Christ as my Savior and Lord, I experienced redemption and started living."

MIKE SIME
"11,000 Days of Surrender and Sobriety"

"Friday, September 18, 1981, was a pretty typical day at Creative Carton. I sold corrugated boxes for the company my dad founded and partially owned. My dad peeked his head into my office, saying, 'Let's go! I want you to come with me to a meeting.' Thinking nothing of it, I grabbed my coffee and we drove one suburb over, to the parking lot of a very nondescript building. Beige, rectangular, and four stories high, with long, thin rectangular windows, the sign by the front door announced that I was walking into the Johnson Institute.

"Dad led me into an interior room that was even more nondescript. The small drab room had bare walls and a few hard chairs placed in a circle. Some were folding chairs, others simple desk chairs. Together, they were an interior decorator's worst nightmare. Walking into the room, I saw my mom, my fiancée, Marcia, and both my siblings—my older sister Suzie and my younger brother Steve—along with a young woman, the counselor, who would serve as the moderator for the intervention. They were sitting in a circle, with two open chairs.

"I knew something was up, but I just couldn't figure out what it was.

"'Mike, everyone is here because they all love you,' the counselor began in a voice that was both soft and authoritative. 'What we'd like to do is to go around the circle, and have each of your family say something to you, one at a time. We would like you to remain quiet, and just listen to what they are saying. Please don't interrupt. Just listen. When they have all had their chance to speak, then you will get your turn to say something.'

"I nodded to her that I understood and agreed. To be perfectly honest, I vividly recall some of the incidents my family recounted that day, but for the life of me I can't remember who said what. But, as they were instructed, each took their turn sharing their concerns.

"'Mike, two months ago we were at the Raspberry Parade together,' one of my family members began in a slow but forceful tone. 'And even early in the day you were already drunk.' I dropped my head, because I knew where this story was going.

"'There were Clydesdale horses in the parade and I can't forget how sad it was when you ran down the street chasing the Clydesdales, yelling to us, 'I want to go pet the horsey!'

"Now I understood what this meeting was all about.

"'Then there was the time you were out driving a mini-bike while you were drunk,' another family member chimed in. 'Thank God the police saw you before you really hurt somebody or hurt yourself. I remember how we had to come down to the police station to bring you home. It was a long drive home, remember? It was a miracle you weren't arrested or charged with anything. But it was frightening, very frightening, nonetheless.'

"Still another family member began to contribute, 'And then there was the time you were out driving Dad's blue Cadillac—do you remember it, Mike?—the navy blue one with the matching leather roof?'

"I nodded weakly and put my head down. This was an especially painful memory.

"'You were drunk and you were driving down the access road by the freeway. The access road had lots of twists and turns, remember? Somehow you made it around the first curve on the frontage road, but had too much speed to make it around the second one. The Cadillac went crashing through the chain link fence that divided the road from the freeway. Dad's car looked like a giant cat clawed it from front to back, top to bottom because of that chain link. I can still remember the roof, with all its fabric ripped from getting sliced up by that fence and the lines scratched into the paint from the hood to the trunk. It's a wonder you didn't kill yourself that night, Mike. Or somebody else.'

"When everyone had said what they had come to say, the counselor turned to me and quietly asked, 'Well, Mike, now that you have heard what all these people who love you have to say to you, do you have anything you want to say in response?'

"I sat quietly in the uncomfortably hard chair in the nondescript room for another moment before opening my mouth. I chose my words carefully and I spoke the truth from my heart. I looked around the room and replied.

"*What took you so long?*'

"The intervention was a relief. I thought I had done a good job of hiding. My drinking never got me arrested. It never caused me to lose a job or even miss a day of work. I wasn't an angry drunk, nor was I an abusive drunk. That's part of why I didn't think I had a problem. In all honesty, I did have a problem and even though it didn't look that way on the outside, I knew on the inside that I was out of control.

"The counselor suggested a five-week treatment program, which included weekly attendance at a meeting of Alcoholics Anonymous. With my wedding scheduled for just three weeks later, the counselor and I agreed that I would enter treatment after Marcia and I were married."

Drinking at Sunset

"It was Sunday evening, October 18, 1981—exactly thirty days since the intervention. I sat alone at our tiny wooden kitchen table, looking out the window as the sun was setting over Lake Minnetonka and thinking about my life. My thoughts were clearer

213

earlier in the evening than they were as the time passed by. For it was true that I was alone, in that no other person was in that room with me. But in another sense, I was not alone. I was accompanied by my constant companion of the last ten years. With me, I had my bottle of scotch. I finished off the nearly full bottle.

"And I continued to think about my life. How did I get to a place where I was the focus of an intervention at age twenty-five? My stomach churned with anxiety as I thought of entering treatment the next day. What's going to happen? The scene faded to black as I passed out, just like I had so many times before.

"And now, I can tell you, it would be the last drink I would have."

Praying at Sunrise

The sunrise was particularly beautiful on the morning that an active 2011 was coming to a close. Now CEO of Rapid Packaging, Mike also held several board leadership positions for the drug and alcohol treatment programs at Hazelden Foundation, The Johnson Institute, and Augsburg College. In addition, he was actively leading the Twin Cities faith community as chair of the 2012 Minnesota Prayer Breakfast.

"We had just moved into our newly built home. As had been my morning ritual for years, I started my day with prayer and reading my favorite devotionals. I remember looking at the beautiful sunrise scene over Lake Minnetonka and asking God, 'What do you want to say to me today?' In my heart I heard, *Pray with your eyes open*. At that moment (and being a bit ADD), I glanced over to my phone. In big letters, it read '11,000 days of sobriety.'

"Oh my gosh!, I thought. It's been more than thirty years since I had my last drink watching the sunset over Lake Minnetonka!"

Mike recalled that first step on his journey, not just toward sobriety, but also toward a life of meaning and purpose. In treatment, Mike learned he was powerless to overcome his alcohol addiction on his own. His only hope was to surrender control to God. It was in Alcoholics Anonymous that Mike made his first spiritual connection to God.

"For me, it's been about the journey and not the destination. Through the years I had learned about God and Jesus, but it wasn't until I discovered that I could have a personal relationship with Jesus that my life made more sense. My world shifted from good to great. Alcoholics Anonymous's twelve steps were like a jigsaw puzzle, where all the pieces began to come together. Each day felt like God had given me a second chance. I became more relaxed and worried less. I began to enjoy life. Over time, little differences started to make a big difference.

"Looking back, I see how God came through every time in spite of my dangerously poor decisions. I feel so blessed that God intervened before I lost everything.

"My journey has fueled my passion for helping people move from addiction to recovery. I also have a passion for people and business. Whenever I get the opportunity to present to business groups, or any group for that matter, no matter what the subject is, I share, 'My name is Mike and I'm an alcoholic. By the grace of God and the help of others, I've been sober since October 18, 1981. For that I'm eternally grateful.'"

CONCLUSION

In the early days of His ministry, Jesus went to His hometown of Nazareth. Arriving at the synagogue to preach, He stood and read the following words from the scroll of the prophet Isaiah: "He has sent me to proclaim freedom for the prisoners and recovery of sight for the blind, to release the oppressed . . ." (Luke 4:18).

Redemption is available to each of us, regardless of our past and present circumstances and choices—to the prisoner, the blind, the oppressed, the cheating executive, the loyal staff member, the alcoholic, the employed, the unemployed . . . you and me. "This righteousness from God comes through faith in Jesus Christ to all who believe. There is no difference, for all have sinned and fall short of the glory of God, and are justified freely by his grace through the redemption that came by Christ Jesus." (Romans 3:22–24).

Redemption is simply the exchange of Christ's life for our freedom. The Merriam-Webster Dictionary defines *redeem* as "to buy back"; or "to free from what distresses or harms, such as to free from captivity by payment of ransom, to release from blame or debt, or to free from the consequences of sin." We think of words that are beyond our ability to achieve, such as ransom, restore, fulfill, clear, exchange, and release.

For some of us, redemption occurs in an instance; for others, it's a process. Regardless, our failings can become stepping-stones to a meaningful and significant life. The God of second chances gives us the freedom we can't earn and don't deserve—freedom to live lives of love, meaning, and purpose. We reflect on Mark's and Mike's stories and recall that despite their individual talents, strengths, and abilities, their redemption was solely the result of God's work in their lives, not their own efforts. As Oswald Chambers writes, "A man cannot redeem himself—redemption is the work of God."[1]

In his book, *Radical*, David Platt writes, "In direct contradiction to the American dream, God actually delights in exalting our inability. He intentionally puts His people in situations where they come face to face with their need for Him. In the process He powerfully demonstrates his ability to provide everything His people need in ways they could never have mustered up or imagined."[2]

In redemption, we discover the most life-changing gift ever given. But how are we to respond? What is our role? What does it mean to be redeemed in our practical day-to-day lives?

Four Responses to a Redeemed Life

Accept God's gift—"Let the peace of Christ rule in your hearts . . ." Colossians 3:15

To "let" the peace of Christ rule in your heart means to accept, receive, or allow it. We've spent a lifetime learning to take control, create action plans, work hard, and achieve goals. For most of us, being in control is much easier than surrendering control. Surrender takes both humility and tremendous courage.

When Mike Sime reached 11,000 days of sobriety, he realized it meant 11,000 days of daily surrender, 11,000 days of God's mercy, and 11,000 days relying on God's power to overcome personal demons. Redemption is a daily gift of God. Accepting it means living a life of faith, trusting God wholeheartedly, and receiving daily peace, regardless of the circumstances of the day.

Be thankful—"Be joyful always; pray continually; give thanks in all circumstances, for this is God's will for you in Christ Jesus." 1 Thessalonians 5:16

Thankfulness is a posture that places perspective on the day. As business people, we often insist on handling difficult situations with our own understanding; we don't feel God will give us what we need to handle life's circumstances. Thankfulness focuses our awareness on God's presence; it's an essential part of our transformation.

In Luke 17, we read of a healing Jesus performs.

As he was going into a village, ten men who had leprosy met him. They stood at a distance and called out in a loud voice, "Jesus, Master, have pity on us!" When he saw them, he said, "Go, show yourselves to the priests." And as they went, they were cleansed. One of them, when he saw he was healed, came back, praising God in a loud voice. He threw himself at Jesus' feet and thanked him—and he was a Samaritan. Jesus asked, "Were not all ten cleansed? Where are the other nine? Was no one found to return and give praise to God except this foreigner?" Then he said to him, "Rise and go; your faith has made you well."

In Charles Dickens's *A Christmas Carol*, Ebenezer Scrooge wakes up Christmas morning absolutely giddy with joy that he was given a second chance. He was transformed from miser to cheerful giver. When we understand the depths of what it means to be saved by God's love and mercy, our nature continues to be transformed as we grow in appreciation of God's love.

Live Free—"It is for freedom that Christ has set us free. Stand firm, then, and do not let yourselves be burdened again by a yoke of slavery." Galatians 5:1

Sometimes, we stay stuck in slavery. We've been forgiven, but we're challenged to forgive others and forgive ourselves. We've been saved by our faith alone, but we continue to try to earn our salvation. We've been given a second chance, but we're stuck in the past, we forfeit the present, and we don't really have hope for a better tomorrow.

Redemption rescues us from our negative thoughts and behaviors. We're still tempted by our nagging, self-defeating thoughts. We still have blind spots that hinder our decisions. We face the burden of guilt, worry, and fear. Our circumstances challenge our thinking. And we still fail. But now we have a choice.

In Deuteronomy 30:19, God tells Moses, "I have set before you life and death, blessings and curses. Now choose life." Redemption gives us the freedom to choose—choose love over hate, peace over worry, joy over discontent, and hope over hopelessness.

Overflow—"God is able to make all grace abound (overflow) to you, so that in all things at all times, having all that you need, you will abound (overflow) in every good work." 2 Corinthians 9:8

A result of your redemption is the overflow of God's grace to the world through you. You can't overflow if you're not first filled. You've been comforted in order to comfort others, received mercy in order to be merciful, forgiven to forgive, and been blessed in order to be a blessing.

The leaders we followed in this chapter, Mark and Mike, walked different paths on the way to redemption. What they have in common is their new sense of purpose to impact the world around them. Mark's commitment and passion is to be a messenger of hope to those who are physically and spiritually oppressed. Mike's second chance has given him a passion to help others become and stay sober. They've embraced their deep sense of calling as a loving response to the God who provided love and grace when it wasn't earned or deserved.

As redeemed followers of Christ, we've been rescued and restored—rescued from our situation and restored to the design that He created us for.

Psalm 40:1–3 paints a beautiful word picture of redemption. "I waited patiently for the Lord; He turned to me and heard my cry. He lifted me out of the slimy pit, out of the mud and mire; He set my feet on a rock and gave me a firm place to stand. He put a new song in my mouth, a hymn of praise to our God."

One of Jesus' names is Immanuel, meaning "God is with us." A friend of mine is going through a challenging time as his wife battles cancer. In one of his daily devotionals, he wrote, "I can't conceive of anything more wonderful than the 'with-ness' of God. A sunset is all the more beautiful being with the One who made it. A fearful situation is more tolerable with the One who holds your future. A sad time is more bearable with the One who will dry every tear. Even a screw-up time is better with God because there is forgiveness and restoration. And for me the best thing is not that God 'was with me' or 'will be with me' but He is with me today."

In the Parable of the Lost Sheep, Jesus describes the shepherd's complete joy in saving the one sheep that strayed from the other ninety-nine.

> And when he finds it, he joyfully puts it on his shoulders and goes home. Then he calls his friends and neighbors together and says, "Rejoice with me; I have found my lost sheep." I tell you that in the same way there is more rejoicing in heaven over one sinner who repents than over ninety-nine righteous persons who do not need to repent. (Luke 15:5–7)

If you're feeling defeated, lost, or alone, take heart! You are in the presence of the God of second chances, who passionately desires to redeem and restore you. Allow Him to transform your surrender into significance.

DISCUSSION GUIDE

1. What thoughts or behaviors enslave you?
2. Are you enslaved because you're having trouble forgiving or asking for forgiveness, or can you identify another cause (such as fear, denial, rationalization, etc.)?

3. Have you fully accepted or are you open to receiving God's gift of redemption? If not, what is holding you back?
4. In Mark 10:51, Jesus asked the blind man, "What do you want me to do for you?" If Jesus asked you this question, what would you want Him to do for you?
5. What is the significance of your redemption?
6. How can you find renewed meaning and purpose moving forward?

Notes

1. Oswald Chambers, as edited by James G. Reimann, *My Utmost for His Highest* (Grand Rapids, MI: Discovery House Publishers, 1992), Devotional October 7.
2. David Platt, *Radical: Taking Back Your Faith from the American Dream* (Colorado Springs, CO: Multnomah Books, 2010), page 47.

11

Timeless Wisdom from Twenty Leaders

God Is My CEO would never have been written had I not had powerful mentors in my life. God blesses and teaches us through others. Paul affirms this when he proclaimed, "We are therefore Christ's ambassadors, as though God was making His appeal through us" (2 Corinthians 5:20). In his final days, Paul shared his most important advice with Timothy, passing God's wisdom on to the next generation's leader.

In the same way, the leaders in this chapter have shared their stories that they might pass what they've learned on to you. The twenty stories that follow are personal and significant and go beyond the bottom line. The profiled leaders are diverse in their style, industry, and life experiences, but are all seasoned and experienced in their professions.

Prepare your heart and mind to receive the individual and collective wisdom of these twenty leaders. Perhaps you'll be inspired, convicted, warned, or encouraged, or experience a mix of these reactions. Within these stories is a message that is specifically for you.

OS GUINNESS
Author, *The Call*

"Calling is the truth that God calls us to Himself so decisively that everything we are, everything we do, and everything we have is invested with a special dynamism, a direction lived out in response to His summons and service.

"In today's world our identity is wrapped up in 'We are what we do.' Calling means 'Do what we are.' We all have a corporate (general) calling, which is our life response to God that we undertake in common with other followers of Christ. But we also have an individual or unique calling. Who has God made you to be? What are your unique gifts, resources, and spheres of influence?

"Cell groups, accountability groups, small group Bible studies, and fellowship groups are crisscrossing America today and that is a positive development. However, there's a missing element—the individuals in the group don't have a clear understanding of each other's callings.

"I challenge you. Learn about each other's callings so you can inspire and encourage each other to pursue their calling. We all face incredible challenges. Pursuing our calling can be very difficult since we are torn in many directions and have many competing distractions. At any given point we need our brothers and sisters to hold our feet to the fire, remind us, and encourage us."

What is your unique calling—who has God made you to be? How can you encourage another to pursue his or her calling?

DENNIS DOYLE
Executive Chairman, Welsh Companies;
Co-Founder, Hope for the City

"**S**ince it began in 2000, Hope for the City has distributed over $575 million in wholesale value of food and supplies. I remember clearly how it started. My wife Megan and I were praying about how our business could be a part of God's plan. We asked ourselves, What's in our hands? What has God given us?

"We came up with three things:

1. We knew a lot of people in the Minneapolis/St. Paul area, particularly CEOs.
2. We owned a lot of commercial real estate, particularly some vacant industrial space.
3. We knew some great ministries and nonprofits that were doing important work, yet needed help.

"We came up with a simple idea. We would go to our CEO friends and get their excesses—things like food, computers, office supplies. Whatever they had, we would put in our vacant warehouse space. Then, once a month, we would have the nonprofits we supported pick up whatever they needed to distribute to the people they serve who are in need.

"What began as a good idea became a God idea! The concept immediately worked, though it was hard work and, especially at the beginning, overwhelming. Megan and I both realized that we had to calm down, wait for God, and allow Him to work on us before we could really get going.

"Looking back, I've learned a lot more than I've ever given out. You start to see God in a whole different dimension when you see how God works through so many people in so many places."

What's in your hands? What (resources, abilities, circumstances) has God given you?

WARD BREHM

Former Chairman, United States African Development Foundation

"**T**wo defining moments have deeply humbled me and transformed my life.

"The first came at forty years old. I was financially successful beyond my wildest dreams. I thought I had figured everything out. And then I went to Africa where I discovered that, as Stephen Covey said, 'I was working hard to climb the ladder of success, only to discover the ladder was leaning against the wrong wall.' I witnessed obscene poverty. It was in Africa I discovered my calling: to be an advocate for people who could not speak for themselves. I will forever be grateful to Africa for humbling me and helping me find meaning and purpose in my work.

"The second defining moment came while sitting in the Mayo Clinic doctor's office with my wife, Kris, and hearing the news that she had three weeks to a month to live. I talk a lot about Jesus and how I love Him and follow Him but if you asked me, 'Do you trust Jesus?' my answer would have been 'I think so, but I don't really know because I've never been in a position where I've had to.' Now I had to. My wife was going to die.

"In the weeks that followed, I discovered what it meant to trust Jesus. First, I witnessed unconditional love like I had never before experienced. It was an unexpected combination of deep sadness and wonderful beauty. I watched as my children overflowed with tears and lavished their mom with expressions of love. Jesus was present. There was no anger, no despair, just acceptance. We were surrounded by a presence of peace unlike anything I've ever understood or experienced.

"Shortly after, we received a miracle. We found a surgeon who was willing to perform an extremely dangerous surgery to remove the cancerous tumor from Kris's fallopian tube . . . and he nailed it. Kris's medical team called this a medical miracle, but stated there was a 70 percent chance the cancer would return. It's been four years and she is still cancer-free. I will be forever grateful to God for humbling me to the point of trusting Jesus and finding peace in the midst of my pain. Everything changed. All the petty little crap that creates arguments and worries went away. It was a wonderful side effect.

"We tend to want to get past the challenges and hardships of our present situation. My advice is to live your life intentionally in the present with a better sense of thankfulness. Thankfulness trumps all the other emotions. You can't be worried, angry, and grumpy and be thankful at the same time. In all your circumstances, good or bad, look for the things to be thankful for.

"And finally, if you could crawl in between the thin lines that are often difficult to discern and even more difficult to stay inside of . . . that's where you find the sweet spot that represents God's calling on your life. It might be finding your Africa or confronting your most challenging problems. If you can find that sweet spot, that's where you find yourself in a place where the Apostle Paul states, 'I have learned the secret of being content in any and every situation, whether well fed or hungry, whether living in plenty or in want. I can do everything through Him who gives me strength.' (Philippians 4:12–13)"

What do you need to do to find your Africa? How have your defining moments helped you find meaning, purpose, peace, and contentment?

RON JAMES
President and CEO, Center for Ethical Business Cultures, University of St. Thomas

"Each of us has been uniquely created for a purpose God has designed for us to fulfill. But we have to be obedient in the moments along the journey. That obedience is reflected in our willingness to listen, learn, and follow God's truth. In each circumstance God places us He creates a unique set of experiences we can learn from. The learning that takes place becomes the foundation for the next step in our journey.

"As a child, my mother was the church pianist, which meant I spent a lot of hours in the church. Initially, I complained, but being nurtured in God's Word at such an early age built my leadership skills. In school, I wanted to be a chemical engineer, only to discover my talents lay in business. In business, my company moved me to a small city, a place my wife and I found challenging. I embraced the opportunity by getting involved with the United Way Campaign, experiencing moments of learning that couldn't have happened in a larger city. Years later, as chair of the 1992 Minneapolis United Way Campaign, I successfully faced great challenges resulting from a national scandal caused by ethical breakdowns. And that learning experience helped prepare me for my current role.

"Enjoy where you are in the moment instead of worrying about the future or regretting the past. When our minds are focused on past mistakes or future plans, we miss out on those precious moments of learning that come from the unique experiences God places before us. In those moments come the experiences that will shape our destiny."

What is your moment of learning right now?

MARC BELTON
Executive Vice President, Global Strategy, Growth and Marketing Innovation, General Mills

"I can't tell you how many times I became a better leader through difficult transformative opportunities that I didn't run from.

"When I was younger, I went through an incredibly difficult divorce. I had little empathy for people struggling with issues because I didn't really appreciate God's grace in my own life. Up to that point, life was easy for me. I took relationships for granted. I couldn't see things from others' perspectives. I certainly didn't appreciate the effort that's required to help people in need. That season of adversity helped set me on a different journey to become a better human being and a better leader. Had I not gone through that I would not be the leader I am today.

"Professionally, I've been in tough vice-grip jobs where all sides tell you you're the zero—even though given the difficulty of the task you should feel like a hero. In one job I was even sent into 'corporate exile.' Interestingly, while in exile, you get a chance to develop true humility, learn new things, and get better. Those times helped me understand what it means to be in His service. I learned how to represent the King by loving and building people, helping company performance by doing things with excellence, and serving the community. All these things reflect well on the company you're serving as well as the One you serve.

"I encourage you: Allow difficult times to transform you. Allow Christ to help you be changed through adversity. You'll be a better leader because of it."

In difficult times, who will you serve and who will you trust? What is God teaching you?

HORST SCHULZE

Chairman and CEO, Capella Hotel Group; Former President and COO, The Ritz-Carlton Hotel Company

"One of the most influential people in my life was a dishwasher. He told me, 'I like to be excellent in all I'm doing.' He taught me not to go to work for work's sake, but to work for excellence in all I do. He showed me that leadership starts with self.

"Leadership implies leading others to a destination. That destination needs to be of value to all concerned. A leader sees something beautiful, excellent, exciting, and worth moving toward.

"First, truly seek God's guidance and ask Him, 'Does this destination serve You and serve others?' Once you see the value and purpose of your vision, there are no excuses. Excuses will get you nowhere. With fortitude and perseverance, move toward your destination no matter what.

"Second, your job as a leader is to see the beauty of the vision and then stimulate the people around you by sharing where you are going and why. Then, with integrity and honor, lead your people by not only setting the course but also by setting a high standard of performance."

What destination are you leading others to? How can you lead with a greater standard of excellence?

AL QUIE
Former Governor and Congressman, State of Minnesota

"As I look back, one of my greatest satisfactions was loving my enemies and having them become my friends. One night I had a life-changing experience. I felt deeply convicted by the Holy Spirit about how I judged my enemies. That experience changed the way I approached people.

"When I was running for governor of Minnesota, I asked myself, If I was elected, who would be the most important Democrat? When I became governor, I went to talk with him, but he wasn't interested in a relationship with me. He became my chief nemesis. I realized that I wanted him to help me, but I wasn't giving anything to him. I asked him, 'What are you trying to accomplish for this country? What are your principles and goals?' My way of loving and giving was to pay attention to his work and ask about him and his purpose. It took time, but we eventually built a solid and trusting friendship.

"Amazing things happen if individuals can operate as Jesus did. We had a small prayer group of Republicans and Democrats—our political views differed greatly. We agreed that Jesus loved us even though we were sinners, so we could love each other in spite of our differing views. We employed 'congenial disputation'—we disputed each other to get to the truth—but we were also courageous enough to be vulnerable, and took the time and commitment to build trusting relationships. We grew to love each other despite our differences."

Who do you need to approach differently? How can you show love to that person today?

ROGER ANDERSEN
Former CEO, Young America Corporation

"Attending Wheaton College was impactful, but was also confusing. I was interested in business and economics while my friends were studying to become pastors and missionaries. I would think, Why didn't I get called? I carried that confusion into my business career. I didn't connect my faith and work at all; they were two totally different spheres. My faith was 'filled up' at church on Sunday and by Wednesday, I was empty. I was living a schizophrenic life. By my early forties, I was successful, but there was something missing.

"I began to research God's purpose for work and the lights came on! Understanding God's purpose for work gave tremendous meaning to my labor. It gave me significance. I saw how God created us as coworkers for His purpose. When I became CEO of Young America Corporation, I saw my responsibility as steward for the owners of the business. Young America was owned in part by private equity firms but was also 40 percent owned by the Ontario Teachers' Pension Plan. I imagined that I was the overseer of the investment dollars of 10,000 teachers. I had a responsibility for their investment, their retirement. I assumed that their quality of life depended on how I ran the company. I also saw myself as a steward for the well-being of each employee (our human assets). What became fulfilling was leading with respect, honesty, and integrity, yet at the same time driving results.

"Like me, many of us think work and worship are two different departments. They are one and the same. Our work is our worship to God."

How do you worship God in your work? How do you find meaning and purpose in your work?

PHIL STYRLUND
CEO, The Summit Group

"In 2009, I had just bought a business, my mom passed away, and the economy evaporated. I was out there grinding away in order to pay the bills. I wore myself down. I was mentally and spiritually exhausted, stopped in my tracks. Up to that point I thought I could outsolve and outwork any problem.

"Am I better for having gone through it? Absolutely! It literally brought me to my knees. I was brought to a place of utter and complete dependence on God. Any pride and hubris I had was stripped away.

"This great humbling helped me to divest myself of lesser activities and invest in things that mattered. I discovered the value of relevance—*mattering to others for others*. I want to serve and impact as many people as I can, and in order to impact people you have to be relevant. There are four drivers to relevance:

1. **Authenticity**—Deep relationships, being vulnerable, sharing my true self, and being real with others helped renew my purpose. Authenticity helps you connect with others on a deeper level.
2. **Mastery**—Adversity helps you understand what you're really good at, but it also helps you get in touch with your limitations. This wisdom gives you resiliency.
3. **Empathy**—Receiving love from people who cared about me more than I cared about myself gave me empathy to connect with others' needs.
4. **Action**—There is no relevance without action. It's the difference between a life of mattering and a life of loitering.

"Relevance matters more than intelligence. By aligning with what people care about, relevance becomes the fuel of significance."

Are you relevant? How can you make a greater impact on the lives around you?

ERIC VERSEMAN
Vice President, Field Supervision, Thrivent Financial

"The first three years I had cancer, my attitude was 'let's deal with it and move on.' It's pretty clear now the end days aren't far away. Cancer has been a catalyst and a blessing; especially the last couple of months. It's helped me realize how precious life is and focus on what matters most.

"I devoted the first fifteen years of my professional life to my work. I realized that working myself to death was no answer to anything. I thought I was working hard for the sake of my wife and kids, but that was just upside down. I missed so many things. I should have been there. What I've learned is don't take anything for granted, particularly your family and friendships.

"While God has blessed my entire life, I've experienced the richness of life more fully the past year than at any other time. I love more purposefully, particularly those closest to me.

"When I started working for Thrivent, I learned about being more purposeful about including God in my work life. It's made such a difference. So if I had one regret, it was not being more bold in my faith at work, particularly the first fifteen years.

"I never gave much thought to how life is an accumulation of small events—events that enhance your quality of life and shape your future. When I announced I was leaving my job to be with my family, I received over 1,000 e-mails! I had no idea! People reached out to share a time I impacted them. Looking back, it was things like a nine-minute conversation, an afternoon meeting, or a brief interaction. All the little things come back later and pay the largest dividends."

*   *   *

Postscript: Eric passed away on August 9, 2013, at fifty-five years of age, just a few weeks after he shared his story with me. I was one of the people Eric impacted the last four years of his life, as I first met him one week after his diagnosis. Here's how he introduced himself:

"I want to thank you for putting on your God Is My Coach seminar. I'm amazed how God works. At your session, I met David Frauenshuh, and he introduced me to the CEO of the Frauenshuh Cancer Center. Right after your seminar, I went for my colonoscopy and learned that I have stage 3 cancer."

My reaction was shock and dread. Eric was cheerful and positive.

Eric became a wonderful friend. Here's the funny thing. I thought if I befriended Eric that I might be able to be a blessing to him. Oh, did I have that backward! For four years, Eric taught me that our response to life's circumstances is a choice. He was consistently positive, ever optimistic, and remarkably appreciative. People would often ask Eric, "How are you doing?" He would answer, "I am blessed." Many were taken aback by his response, especially as time grew closer to the end. Eric knew where he was going, so "he was blessed."

Eric's funeral exuded joy. Having time to prepare for it, Eric chose his favorite songs and Bible verses. So on a warm August day, we sang "Joy to the World" and listened to Louis Armstrong's "What a Wonderful World."

The Greek words for *joy* mean "awareness of God's grace" and "grace recognized." Eric's life was about joy—receiving God's grace and allowing it to overflow to others. Love trumped fear. Purpose trumped pain. Hope trumped uncertainty. Joy reigned.

Our lives are but a breath. What changes do you need to make today to make your life more purposeful and meaningful?

JERRY COLANGELO

Former Owner, the Phoenix Suns and the Arizona Diamondbacks

"**M**y most challenging times taught me to trust in Jesus and that God has a plan for my life. As a successful college athlete, I had big dreams, but injuries ended my sports career. At twenty-six, things looked bleak. I wasn't sure what the next day would bring.

"When you're humbled, you learn that you aren't capable of handling adversity on your own. I learned to seek God's guidance even when things didn't make sense.

"My success in the business world, for example, didn't make sense on paper, but God had a plan. During the tough times, I maintained my relationship with Jesus. I was consistent with who I was. Looking back, I've learned more from my mistakes and setbacks than I did my successes. I've played out God's game plan to the best of my ability.

"Ironically, my playing career ended in college, but I've been privileged to serve the Phoenix community through sports—through the Phoenix Suns and Arizona Diamondbacks—and represent our country through the United States Olympic Basketball Team.

"Too often people complain about their situation and wallow in their misery. As a result, they don't see the opportunity before them. My advice is to maintain your integrity. Even when things look hopeless, be open to the opportunities before you."

What before you seems impossible or hopeless? What small steps can you take to explore the possibilities within those impossibilities?

KEN BLANCHARD
Chief Spiritual Officer, The Ken Blanchard Companies; Author, *The One Minute Manager*

"**M**y life's defining moment came from a success rather than a failure. *The One Minute Manager* was so ridiculously successful (over 13 million copies sold) that it ignited my faith. I realized there must be someone else in control. When I wrote *The One Minute Manager*, I wasn't a believer, but I look back and see God's hand on my life. After the book was published, people began to share with me how Jesus was the ideal one-minute manager. God opened doors to great people who helped me on my journey toward knowing Jesus on a deep level.

"The world's definition of success is money, power, recognition, and status. Significance is the opposite; it's about service and loving relationships. If you focus on success, you'll never get to significance. Success *follows* significance. Consider Mother Teresa, for example. Mother Teresa wasn't concerned about money or recognition. She was all about service, generosity, and loving relationships, and yet, across the globe, people fell over each other trying to give her money, recognition, and status.

"Keep your eye on God's court, with an intention of glorifying God. You glorify Him by creating loving, caring relationships with your employees so they can create loving, caring relationships with your customers. That gives you success.

"The key attribute of a great leader is humility. People with humility don't think less of themselves; they just think about themselves less. Great leaders realize that leadership isn't about them, but about the people they're trying to influence. That's done through true humility, which is the antidote to false pride. It's also the antidote to fear and self-doubt. A lot of leaders who are self-serving are like scared little kids. I don't think you can make people around you feel good about themselves if you don't feel good about yourself. That's where trust in the unconditional love of the Lord is really important.

"I often say to people in my audience, 'How many of you love your kids?' Every parent raises a hand. Then I continue, 'How many of you love your kids only if they're successful?' Not one hand goes up. I would ask, 'You mean you love your kids unconditionally? Then why wouldn't you trust God the Father? He loves you unconditionally.'

"With the understanding that we are unconditionally loved by God, when our performance isn't good or people are upset with us, we can say, 'I wonder what we can do to turn this performance around? Could you tell me more about what I have done that upsets you?' Bottom line, our self worth isn't the issue because we're unconditionally loved. We're okay, but we also know we can learn because we're not perfect.

"In the end, humility is the driver. It's not about you. All the great leaders get that. If you get out of your own way and realize you're here to serve and not be served, it's amazing what kinds of things can happen."

In what ways can you prioritize significance over success? How does knowing that you're unconditionally loved change your response to feedback?

KEN SANDE

Founder, Peacemaker Ministries; President, Relational Wisdom 360; Author, *The Peacemaker*

"'Building passport' is relating to people in such a way that they allow you to come deeper and deeper into their lives. You're able to move past the superficial façade we all put up and really get to know them—their strengths, weaknesses, victories, and fears. People won't just allow you to come into their lives; they're very selective—you have to earn that privilege.

"In the back of their minds, people are usually asking three questions:

1. Can I trust you?
2. Do you really care about me or love me?
3. Can you really help me?

"Successful businesses are built on relationships of trust. Building a team with a high level of trust is crucial to individual and team success. The same is true with customers and vendors. If we really and sincerely look out for the interests of others—their personal interests, business interests, and financial interests—and treat them the way we ourselves want to be treated, the vast majority of people will treat us the same way.

"Investing, listening, caring, and making some sacrifices along the way for them will generally return to us the blessing of real friendship, real trust, and real respect. Those qualities are enormously valuable, both personally and in the business world.

"Ask yourself, 'How do I want to be treated?' The thought of having someone care for me, listen to me, understand me, and look out for my interests is appealing. If that's what I want, then I want to do that for others. It's a simple but powerful compass that changes relationships."

How can you build passport with those people with whom you desire a deeper relationship?

DAVID FRAUENSHUH
CEO and Founder, Frauenshuh, Inc.

"**M**y first job was leasing and managing office space for a building in downtown St. Paul, Minnesota. I earned a starting wage, just making ends meet, but with the pending sale of the building I managed, I didn't know how I would continue to support my family. During that time of uncertainty, one Sunday morning the pastor announced that the church was in need of money. I leaned over to Sandy and whispered, 'I think we need to put a hundred dollars in the plate.' Sandy and I looked at each other, realizing we didn't have the money. We took the leap of faith and I wrote a check on ready reserve.

"The next morning, a man walked into my office and said, 'You don't know me, but I work for the bank across the street. We're looking for a new property manager and would like to offer you the job.'

"On Sunday, I wrote out a check for $100 and on Monday, I was offered a job with a substantial raise that allowed me to cover the check and then some.

"I realized that it was God's money, not mine. From that point forward I focused on being a good steward. I sought God's wisdom in all my business transactions. I feel the Lord has taken me by the hand and helped me make wise business decisions.

"I've become successful doing the simple things. Being dependable. Paying loans back on time. Doing the right thing. Making financially sound decisions. Being open and honest in my transactions. Investing in people.

"Doing these things doesn't guarantee financial success, but the Lord will reward your stewardship in many ways."

How do you honor God with your financial decisions?

LESLIE FRAZIER
Head Coach, Minnesota Vikings

"**M**odeling faith starts at home. My kids need to see a father who loves Jesus Christ, who will pray, be vulnerable, and who can communicate and not feel it has to be my way. They need to see Jesus through their father. My wife needs to know she has a loving, forgiving husband who will honor and respect her. That's very important to me.

"Growing up without a father and with a mother who wasn't around was difficult. And yet, we have a lot of players whose background is similar to mine. Probably 60–70 percent of our players grew up in a single-parent home. I'm very conscious of the fact that many of our players did not grow up with a male authority at home. I know my role is bigger than just being their coach and communicating x's and o's.

"I have to model the right way to treat people, how to deal with confrontation, and how to treat my wife, for example. I understand my impact—especially as an African American male with a family—on this generation of players, and I recognize what it can mean to some of our players who come into contact with me daily.

"It's important for me to model consistency and the character of Christ, to serve people around me, and to be selfless. I want to be an example as a leader. I was hired to win a championship in Minnesota, and I want to win that championship with high character guys."

Do you model your faith in the way you desire? At home? At work?

TAD PIPER
Retired Chairman and CEO, Piper Jaffray Companies

"Find your inspiration. There are two components to inspiration: to be inspired and to be inspiring.

"If you're just starting your career, you need to find something that drives you forward that's more than a paycheck. A paycheck may be motivational, but it isn't inspiring. Pursue things that are meaningful. Open yourself up and actively look to be inspired by your faith, a mission, or someone you admire. Be willing to invest the time and energy to find God's calling upon your life.

"If you're already a leader, you need to be inspiring. Make sure your mission has purpose and meaning beyond the bottom line. Give your employees a reason to get up in the morning and do something that matters—something that matters to them, the people they work with, their customers, and society.

"As capable as you are (or as you think you are), you can't lead an organization on your own. If you're inspirational, you'll have a lot of people who want to work *with* you, which is much better than having people work *for* you. We all want to be a part of something bigger than ourselves.

"Leadership sets the tone of an organization. Lead by example. How you behave, the words you use, and how you treat others are all part of being inspirational. If you're too safe, life isn't nearly as rich or enjoyable. Find your inspiration and live it out with passion. You'll have more fun."

What inspires you? How do you inspire others?

BRAD HEWITT
CEO, Thrivent Financial

"Early on as a CEO, I was driven to win and succeed. Jet-lagged, I had little left to give my family. The turning point was a Saturday morning when my wife, Sue, asked me to watch our three-year-old daughter so she could run errands. Our daughter cried, 'I don't want to be with Daddy!' She didn't know me. I was a stranger. I had never given her the gift of time and I deeply felt the sting of my lack of generosity.

"Generosity was as natural for me as jumping in front of a train. It seemed downright impossible. I've since discovered that generosity's benefits far outweigh the benefits of selfishness. As I think of times I've given to someone, I benefited more. Generosity has the amazing power to stimulate contentment, joy, and peace.

"I see my purpose as starting a revolution of generosity—helping families be wise with their money and inspiring them to be generous. God has a sense of humor—taking the stingiest person on earth and asking him to encourage others toward generosity!

"In terms of attributes I seek in a leader, I facetiously say, 'I look for left-handed musicians!' My musician friends tend to be left-handed and have two traits I value greatly—discipline and creativity. Discipline is combining hard work and practice. Creativity is looking at things differently. However, there's a third trait that makes the other two work effectively together—humility. With creativity and discipline, you can be successful for a while, but not the long run. Humility gives leaders the perseverance to lead in good times and bad."

Whom do you need to be generous with today? How can you enhance your "left-handed leader" traits?

MARILYN CARLSON NELSON
Former Chairman and CEO, Carlson

"I've always considered the opportunity to lead Carlson as a calling. Imagine the gratification of knowing that our family-owned business has provided jobs from entry level to lifelong careers for millions of people and their families for seventy-five years! After all, the greatest philanthropy is a job. Leading a global company has also given me the opportunity to lead with love, as my faith asks of me. But I do confess, it has 'exercised' my faith in both challenging and rewarding ways.

"I felt I was leading with love when we needed to downsize significantly during a severe economic downturn. Someone asked me if I had the heart to do this. 'No, I don't have the heart,' I replied, 'but I have the head.' I knew it was necessary for the long-term survival of the company and the employees who would remain. I could only hope that one day, those who had to leave might return . . . and many did.

"I'm quite sure that my leadership is also influenced by being raised in the Methodist Church. The church's founder, John Wesley, said this:

> Do all the good you can,
> By all the means you can,
> In all the ways you can,
> In all the places you can,
> To all the people you can,
> As long as ever you can.

"Talk about 'asking for the order!' But the truth is, leading with love does ask a lot of us. Sometimes it is tough, courageous, lonely love. But more often, it is thoughtful, creative, caring, and rewarding love. As we all know, the world is hungry for this kind of leadership."

Can people see your faith through how you lead?

JEANNINE M. RIVET
Executive Vice President, UnitedHealth Group

"**M**ost people don't change, but you can. Changing the tone and the dialogue can open up productive, meaningful communication.

"Several years ago, our organization acquired a large company, requiring us to reorganize. I approached our CEO and told him, 'I'm willing to do whatever job you want me to do to support the organization.' He appreciated that approach, and I soon took on an expanded role. Rather than focusing on how I could succeed, I was open to new opportunities, whatever they may be.

"A big part of changing the dialogue is how you talk to people. In difficult conversations, people often become angry or fearful. It's easy to get caught up in the negative dialogue that can follow. But if you shift your focus to a positive one, people will respond positively; they'll become more engaged and their energy level will go up.

"One time I was in challenging negotiations with a physicians' group. Our negotiations had hit the wall. People had become angry, defensive, and simply wouldn't talk. The next morning I came to the meeting with a bag of tomatoes and placed it at the center of the U-shaped table. I stood in front of them wearing a flak jacket and said, 'I don't know what's on your mind but feel free to throw the tomatoes and get it out of your system!' Stunned, they began to laugh. As radical as it seemed, my approach told them that I wanted to enter into productive dialogue."

When you need to have a meaningful conversation, particularly when the subject is sensitive or adversarial, how can you change the dialogue and move the conversation toward a positive outcome?

RICHARD STEARNS
President, World Vision U.S.

"You might imagine a person who leads a large, global humanitarian organization that feeds the hungry, assists disaster victims, and cares for widows and orphans across the planet to be some kind of spiritual hero or saint. You are sorely mistaken. I was a most reluctant recruit to this cause—in many ways a coward.

"In my prayers over the weeks leading up to my appointment as World Vision's president, I begged God to send someone else to do it. As CEO of Lenox, the fine china company, I was living the American dream—I had a prestigious job with financial wealth and a ten-bedroom home on five acres of land.

"The headhunter representing World Vision wanted to meet with me, but I refused. Then he asked a powerful question: 'Are you willing to be open to God's will for your life?'

"God was asking me that day to choose. He was challenging me to decide what kind of disciple I was willing to be. What was the most important thing in my life? Was it my career, my financial security, my family, the Jaguar XK8, my stuff? Or was I committed to following Him regardless of the cost—no matter what?

"Not long after, I sat in my kitchen and thought, What if there are children who will suffer somehow because I failed to obey God? What if my cowardice costs even one child somewhere in the world his or her life?

"From the beginning, my wife Reneé had said, 'We need to be where God wants us to be, and if that's at World Vision, we will just go.'

"In April, I officially accepted the board's invitation.

"In May, I resigned as CEO of Lenox.

"In June, I started my new job as World Vision's U.S. president.

"In July, the moving van pulled up to our two-hundred-year-old fieldstone farmhouse.

"And in August, I was in the jungles of Uganda, with a boy and his orphaned brothers. I wondered if that boy was the one child I had worried about in my kitchen that night so long ago, the one who might die if I disobeyed God. I think God was showing me that he was.

"That God still chooses to use flawed human beings like me is both astonishing and encouraging. And if He can use me, He can use you."

How is God calling you to move from belief to action? What kind of disciple are you willing to be?

Story excerpted from *The Hole in Our Gospel* by Richard Stearns. Reprinted by permission. *The Hole in Our Gospel*, 2009, Richard Stearns, Thomas Nelson Inc. Nashville, Tennessee. All rights reserved.

OBSERVATIONS FROM THE CUTTING ROOM FLOOR

Asked to summarize Leo Tolstoy's classic novel, *War and Peace*, comedian Woody Allen exclaimed, "It's about Russia!" That's a little how I feel about the task of summarizing the lessons and wisdom shared by these twenty leaders. While I wanted to capture each leader's most important message in a concise way, I never imagined the depth of insight and meaning that would be left on the cutting room floor.

This creates an interesting dilemma. On one side, the brevity of each message conveys its importance, yet it runs the risk of being perceived as a mere platitude, simply because of space limitations that prevent us from sharing the rest of each leader's story.

As the messenger for these stories, I've had the privilege of gaining deeper insight into the individual behind each message. The leaders profiled here arrived at their messages in a multitude of ways, none of which was easy. Beyond what we gain from their individual teachings, I believe we can also learn from the nature of the group. I've found the twenty leaders share four similar characteristics—and they are, in fact, four crucial character qualities of successful leaders: humility, courage, faithfulness, and love.

Humility

When a leader demonstrates humility and surrenders control to God, God transforms their leadership and uses it to change the course of the leader's life.

- Through the humbling Africa provided, Ward Brehm discovered his calling: to be an advocate for people who could not speak for themselves. In the process, Ward found meaning and purpose in his work.

- With a focus on stewardship and doing the simple things right, David Frauenshuh became successful by seeking God's wisdom in all his business decisions.
- When God asked him to choose what kind of disciple he was willing to be, Richard Stearns left a comfortable, prestigious job to serve the needs of the world's disaster victims and the poor through World Vision.

Courage

It can be difficult to see the opportunity amongst the obstacles. The external pressure for results combined with the internal temptations that come with power, money, and position can be overwhelming. Courage enables a leader to follow God's call in spite of the counterinfluences.

- Os Guinness reminds us that calling doesn't mean *we are what we do*. Calling means *do what we are*. Who has God made you to be? What are your unique gifts, resources, and spheres of influence?
- Courage allowed Brad Hewitt to face his stinginess head-on and for it to be overcome with a new calling—to encourage others toward generosity.
- Ron James discovered that valuable moments of learning come from the unique experiences God places before us, and it's in those moments that our lives are enriched.
- To overcome their political differences and get to the truth, Al Quie's prayer group relied on "congenial disputation," combined with the courage to be vulnerable and build trusting relationships with one another.
- For Jeannine Rivet, courage means being open to change, and that change results in productive and meaningful communication.

Faithfulness

Faithful leaders persevere in adversity and remain true to their calling, even when it conflicts with conventional wisdom. Successful leaders exhibit loyalty, faithfulness, and a steadfast love of God and others through the ups and downs of life.

- Marc Belton returned from "corporate exile" and a season of adversity as a more empathetic human being and a better leader.
- During the tough times, Jerry Colangelo was consistent about who he was. He's able to look back and realize he learned more from his mistakes and setbacks than from his successes.
- Phil Styrlund's great humbling helped him to divest himself of lesser activities and discover the value of relevance—mattering to others for others.
- Eric Verseman entered into eternal glory after a four-year journey with cancer. Eric was the epitome of persevering in adversity, and discovered the simple joy of understanding that life is an accumulation of small events—events that enhance your quality of life and shape your future.

Love

Love is leading with a purpose greater than the bottom line. True leadership is a purpose-driven calling, not an outcome-driven task.

- Roger Andersen became driven to understand God's purpose for work and discovered that we are coworkers for His purpose and stewards of what we're given.
- Ken Blanchard teaches how being unconditionally loved impacts who we are. A thriving leader focuses on

significance—service and loving relationships—and finds that success follows.

- For Marilyn Carlson Nelson, faith is love in action, and leading with love means stepping up and taking action for the greater good.
- Dennis and Megan Doyle prayed about how their business could be a part of God's plan. The result is a vibrant organization that's distributed over $575 million in goods to those in need.
- As a role model to his young players, Leslie Frazier focuses on serving others with the consistency and character of Christ.
- Tad Piper motivates through inspiration—a leader must be both inspired and inspiring; people need to do something that matters.
- Ken Sande teaches how to "build passport" by relating to people in such a way that they allow you to come deeper and deeper into their lives. Investing, listening, caring, and making sacrifices along the way returns to us the blessing of real friendship, real trust, and real respect.
- Horst Schulze leads by understanding the value and purpose of his vision, and then setting the course and leading with integrity, honor, and high standards.

The leadership characteristics of humility, courage, faithfulness, and love visibly flow from these twenty stories and messages. But what's more striking than what they have in common is the individual nature of each leader's personal story and message. As we revisit each story, we can't help but notice how unique each leader is. Each leader's advice and message is based on his or her experiences and personal story.

And isn't that how God created us—and you? You've been fashioned by an almighty God with a unique personality and style, specific life experiences, circumstances, obstacles, and opportunities—all to shape you into the leader He desires you to be.

So take this wisdom you've gleaned, whether it be an encouragement or an admonishment, an inspiration or a warning, and allow these insights to influence who you are as a leader. Regardless of the challenges you face, remember God's promise in Jeremiah 29:11. "For I know the plans I have for you," declares the Lord, "plans to prosper you and not to harm you, plans to give you hope and a future."

As Richard Stearns of World Vision expresses so well, "That God still chooses to use flawed human beings like me is both astonishing and encouraging. And if He can use me, He can use you."

Conclusion

A Message of Hope

Our future is determined by what we believe and do. Every one of our beliefs generates behavior, and every behavior has a consequence. Ultimately, *we become what we believe and do every day.* As we did at the beginning of this book, we can ask ourselves: What are the beliefs that drive our business decisions? Does our faith define who we are at work, or do the business rules define who we are? Are we on the right path?

When you integrate God's principles along with your unique talents, skills, and character, you create a powerful partnership for being successful *in* the world without becoming *of* the world. As a result, your challenges and dilemmas strengthen you to become the successful and significant leader God intended you to be.

What characterizes us as godly leaders? Pressure strengthens us, prioritizing principles over profits enhances our value over time, our character is made stronger over time, and, finally, we produce a legacy, in addition to bottom-line results. At the core of our quest for meaningful work is a clash between two masters. In the end, we need to choose.

Walking with God while facing and overcoming life's difficulties is absolutely invaluable to a person—both personally and professionally. Each of the thirty-five leaders profiled in these pages understood that difficulty is a part of life and that God communicates to us through our circumstances, especially the difficult ones. Each leader also recognized that we can't check God at the door when we go to work. Our work consumes at least half of our waking life. How can we exclude God from half of our life and be personally and professionally successful? Finally, these leaders pursued those things deemed excellent and worthy, regardless of the difficulty faced.

In his valuable book, *My Utmost for His Highest*, Oswald Chambers said, "All efforts of worth and excellence are difficult. Difficulty does not make us faint and cave in—it stirs us up to overcome. God does not give us overcoming life—*He gives us life as we overcome.*"[1]

The essence of the stories shared in this book is that we grow closer to God through our difficulties and dilemmas, one decision at a time. To close, I would like to share the process that defines our success, our purpose for seeking God, and His promise for our reward.

The Process

> *We rejoice in our sufferings, because we know that suffering produces perseverance;*
> *perseverance, character; and character, hope.*
> *And hope does not disappoint us, because God has poured out his love into our hearts by the Holy Spirit, whom he has given us.*
> —Romans 5:3–5

In 1999, while writing the original *God Is My CEO*, I experienced great personal and professional difficulties. Monty Sholund, my Bible study teacher, counseled me through every difficult trial and situation.

Consistently, Monty's advice to me was, "Don't miss out on the privilege of your problems." I would share my challenges with him, and inevitably, he would comment, "Oh, this is sooo valuable!" Without minimizing my pain, he would share the value of learning and growing closer to God from all circumstances, no matter how difficult.

The leaders who shared their stories with us have each struggled with a difficult dilemma, decision, or situation. Each had the ability to use his or her particular situation or dilemma for his or her growth. In essence, their problems weren't stumbling blocks, but stepping-stones for personal growth and success. In the same way, the decisions we make in the midst of our dilemmas define us. They shape our character, and they determine our destiny. They are, in short, our journey.

As we struggle, we can choose to focus not on the pain of our present situation, but on the value of the moment. The problems we each face are our own opportunities. Our present situations are part of a much larger process. They are leading us, step by step, to the place God wants us to be.

Our Purpose

> *O Lord Almighty, blessed is the man who trusts in You.*
> —Psalm 84:12

Trust in the Lord is a trait common to the thirty-five leaders in this book. At some point, these leaders took a leap of faith, not knowing what the outcome would be. Each had fears, doubts, and difficulties, yet they each came to a defining moment where they trusted in God more than they trusted in their own understanding of the situation. This moment of faith played a significant role in shaping the destiny of their lives. In the same way, a time will come when our faith will be tested to the limit—a time when business pressure, intellectual logic, and fear gang up to the point where an easier business decision makes more sense to us than trusting God. This may be the greatest spiritual crisis we will ever face, a point where it is no longer a moral or ethical business decision, but a battle of wills. In fact, choosing God's will may go completely against our business reasoning and may cost us money, a promotion, or even a career. The decision we make is one of our will for our life versus God's will for our life.

At this point, we need to take whatever time is needed to pray for God's guidance. Once we know in our heart what God is calling us to do, we need to trust Him and take that leap of faith. Then He can work.

His Promise

No eye has seen, no ear has heard, no mind has conceived what God has prepared for those who love Him.

—1 Corinthians 2:9

We live in a business world that measures success. With every business decision, we calculate a return on investment, a profit margin, or a return on shareholder equity. In doing so, we sell ourselves short. By trying to maximize a return based on what we know, we don't allow ourselves to imagine what can be. God has promised us wonderful things beyond our imagination if only we believe His promises.

Our profiled leaders don't necessarily have happier lives, but they do live lives filled with personal meaning. They've also made a difference in other people's lives. God doesn't promise us happy, carefree lives, filled with timely job promotions and lots of amenities. He promises Himself. As Monty Sholund explains, "God is enough. He is the reward of those who seek Him."

Personally, there would have been no way I would have written this book if I had relied solely on my thoughts and desires. In understanding the time, energy, hassles, pain, problems, and dilemmas that went into the writing process, I would have quickly determined that it wasn't worth the effort. The tangible return on investment simply didn't make sense.

However, as I write the last words of this book, I know that I've already been blessed beyond my imagination. I've been blessed by the stories of these remarkable leaders, and I've been blessed by a closer relationship with God. Those dividends are beyond measure.

My prayer is that this book has helped you think about God and His plan for your life. God loves you and wants you to prosper. He has prepared something for you that is beyond comprehension now, but will be revealed to you over time. May God bless you on your journey.

Notes

1. Oswald Chambers, as edited by James G. Reimann, *My Utmost for His Highest* (Grand Rapids, MI: Discovery House Publishers, 1992), Devotional July 7.

APPENDIX
Your Personal Business Plan

Introduction

"For I know the plans I have for you," declares the Lord, "plans to prosper you and not to harm you, plans to give you hope and a future. Then you will call upon me and come and pray to me, and I will listen to you. You will seek me and find me when you seek me with all your heart."

—Jeremiah 29:11–12

The messages bombard us daily: "You can have it all." "You can make it happen." Motivational speakers promise, "Create your own destiny" and offer countless ways to help us achieve our plans for financial success. What happens? We rejoin the rat race with all its pressures. Then, when trouble knocks on our door, we call on God to solve *our* problems. When He doesn't fix our situation, we think God is punishing us. The real issue is that our plan itself was flawed. While it may have been our plan for success, it was never God's plan. It was doomed from the beginning.

God's plan for you is *specifically designed for your success*. He's called you by name to fulfill His plan for your life. God has defined success His own way, not the world's way; and He's provided a plan for you to succeed His way, not your way; and on His timing, not yours. While this sounds harsh, it's important to challenge your thinking before you begin to create your business plan. Following God's plan is not a part-time pursuit, but a full-time commitment. Take a moment to re-read the last sentence of Jeremiah 29:11–12: "You will seek me and find me when you seek

265

me with all your heart." Are you willing to trust God with all your heart, even during those tough times when nothing seems to be going right? If you're ready to answer "yes," then let's get started.

Your personal business plan is based on three principles and a promise. By following these principles, we become like the tree planted by streams of water in Psalm 1:3: We yield fruit, grow strong, and prosper in all we do.

Three Principles and a Promise: Realizing God's Plan

He is like a tree planted by streams of water, which yields its fruit in season and whose leaf does not wither. Whatever he does prospers.

—Psalm 1:3

Principle #1: God is the source of our wisdom, strength, and energy.

The most important relationship we have is private and ongoing— our daily relationship with the Lord. The first step in every decision and action is to seek God's wisdom. By following Principle #1, our roots—the roots of the tree that reach deep into the ground—find streams of living water. These streams of living water represent God's wisdom. This relationship is the nourishment for all we do.

Principle #2: Our personal plan is a plan for growth, not a plan for achieving things.

Just as a tree produces more fruit as it matures, we need to grow spiritually in order to live a life of abundance. Most people who fail to follow through on their plans do so because of immaturity. Faced with frustration or fear, they quickly abandon their plans when things don't go as planned. Our personal business plans are a means to grow in the right direction as we respond to life's changes and storms. Principle #2 represents our character growth as we work our plans. Think of this as the trunk and branches of the tree, being shaped by constantly changing conditions. The branches bend with the winds and the trunk grows stronger in harsh winters. The tree grows stronger as it weathers each storm.

Principle #3: We will enjoy success in God's timing.

In a society that demands immediate gratification, waiting on God's timing can be painful. Since *God Is My CEO* was first published in 2002, I've been blessed more than I could have imagined. God has used the book to change lives, providing me with tremendous fulfillment as I watch the fruits of my labor.

Looking back, however, I clearly remember the seven years when I sacrificed money, time, and energy and received neither compensation nor "pats on the back" for the manuscript that would become *God Is My CEO*. This waiting period was often painful, and filled with professional defeat and personal loss. God promises us that, in season, the tree will bear fruit. I believe it was the length and difficulty of the journey that produced the sweetness of the fruit I later experienced.

Finally, the Promise: Prosperity

As a byproduct of working with your personal business plan, you may experience successes, such as a rewarding job or a financially profitable business. I believe that working your plan will increase your likelihood of financial success. However, God does not promise us financial success, nor does He promise to spare us from pain, suffering, or defeat. What does God promise? He promises Himself. With His presence, He provides rewards beyond our imagination. It's a journey worth taking.

One Last Note

Before you begin the journey, I need to make one important point. While ultimately your plan *will* succeed, it won't be devoid of adversity. The difficulties you encounter are important because they contribute to your growth. The greatest obstacles to your success are not circumstances, but fears and discouragements that cause you to abandon your plan. God gives us a powerful message in Joshua 1:9: "Have I not commanded you? Be strong and courageous. Do not be terrified: do not be discouraged, for the Lord your God will be with you wherever you go."

I can't tell you how many times I wanted to abandon my plans for writing *God Is My CEO*. I constantly battled fear and discouragement. I made a lot of mistakes, and wanted to quit over and over. But God never quit on me or left me; He was with me wherever I went. I want to encourage you to have the courage needed to find God's calling in your life. Though you may stumble, remember He is with you through it all. God bless you and enjoy the journey!

How to Write Your Personal Business Plan

In the pages that follow, you will develop your personal business plan, step by step. Your personal business plan will include the following components:

1. Your situational analysis
2. Your vision
3. Your core values and principles
4. Your mission
5. The need
6. Your unique quality
7. The target market
8. An environment for growth

9. Your products and services
10. Your strategic partnerships
11. Your personal, professional, and spiritual development plan
12. Your sales and marketing plan
13. Your financial plan
14. The fruit
15. Renewal

God is speaking to us all the time, constantly revealing His plans for us. Instead of yelling to get our attention, however, God whispers our name. In order to hear His call, we must retreat from the busyness of life and quiet our souls. To begin the journey of creating your personal business plan, quiet yourself before God.

For each component of the plan, I'll ask some thought-provoking questions and give you several action items to make the writing process easier and your words more effective. Then, you'll summarize your approach to each component. Once you've written each piece, you'll have a complete personal business plan.

Using Your Personal Business Plan

I've been creating business plans for more than thirty years and have seen many of them fail. Some people give complete responsibility for their lives to God and assume no accountability for their own actions (or inaction) and decisions (or indecision). These people drift through life with no direction or purpose. Others run ahead of God trying to do everything on their own. They charge ahead only to find that they have expended tremendous effort to go down the wrong path. A successful personal business plan is a partnership with God, a daily walk with God one decision at a time, one day at a time.

The Gift

God's gift to you is His grace and His plan for you to prosper. Your gift to God is your character: how you grow closer to Him as you follow His plan. Your partnership with God is a gift to others: the fruit you produce and the legacy you leave.

This workbook and personal business plan is intended as a tool to help you fulfill God's plan. It is a framework or guideline, not a formula. Above all, remember that the plan is more about the journey than the outcome. The process itself, not the outcome, glorifies God.

Working the Plan a Day at a Time

I heard the voice of the Lord saying, "Who shall I send, and who will go with us?" Then I said, "Here am I! Send me."
—Isaiah 6:8

One of the most profound things Marilyn Carlson Nelson, former chairman and CEO of Carlson, has taught me is the concept of making the most of each day. She asks, "Are you willing to put your signature on this day?" God doesn't force us to do His will. Rather, He gives us complete freedom to choose.

Four attitudes will help us make each day our signature day:

1. *Appreciation* Lord, thank you for the gift of this day. Regardless of circumstances, good or bad, I thankfully accept all that is in this day.
2. *Availability* I'm totally available to You and, therefore, available to others.
3. *Awareness* I understand You communicate through the people and circumstances that surround me. I further rec-

ognize that the closer I come to you, the more I can hear Your whisper through people and circumstances. Therefore, I commit to my awareness of Your presence over the busyness of life.

4. *Alignment* My goal is to be one with You. Every decision I make and all I do reflects your nature.

Seven Reminders

In our efforts to make each day our signature day, these seven reminders will help keep us focused on our plans:

1. *Perspective* God sees what we can't. Don't deduce that your plan is failing because you've had a bad day. God wastes nothing; He uses everything for His plan. Trust that this day is part of a much larger plan that will bear fruit in the proper time.

2. *Purpose* It's His purpose, not yours. Be flexible to adjust your plans according to His purpose.

3. *Priority* Keep the important things important.

4. *Process* The process—not the outcome—glorifies God. Along the way, you may find life won't fit into your plan. Your plan needs to evolve with life.

5. *Patience and Perseverance* It's His timing, not yours. God uses everything, even suffering, for His purpose. Trust that your perseverance is preparing you for greater service to Him. As Jean Jacques Rousseau observed, "Patience is bitter, but its fruit is sweet."

6. *Peace* God never calls us to maximize work; He calls us to meaningful work. Deliberately take time daily to rest in Him. It will give you the energy to work both effectively and meaningfully.

7. *Prosperity* While each day won't show signs of success, each day is significant. At the end of the day, reflect on its positive aspects and thank God for His blessings.

Exploring the Parts of the Business Plan

1. Your Situational Analysis

Are you familiar with the saying *success leaves clues*? Well, that's half right—success does leave clues. But so does failure. As part of the creation of our plan, we want to both build on our successes and learn from our failures. To complete your situational analysis, quiet yourself before God and review the past year's work.

THOUGHT-PROVOKING QUESTIONS

What's working? What were my specific successes and achievements over the past year?

....

What's not working? What were my frustrations and disappointments?

....

Conduct a brief S.W.O.T. analysis: Identify your strengths, weaknesses, opportunities, and threats.

Strengths: *I'm good at:*

....

....

Weaknesses: *These things hinder my performance:*

....

....

Opportunities: *The biggest opportunities I'm sitting on right now appear to be:*

....

....

Threats: *The greatest threats facing me right now are:*

....

....

What valuable insights can I gain from the successes and challenges of the past year?

....

....

ACTION PLAN

❑ Review your weekly planner for the previous twelve months. To help gain insights for your situational analysis, highlight your successes and frustrations.

❑ Ask a friend, family member, coworker, pastor, or customer to review and discuss your S.W.O.T. analysis with you. Choose to be open to his or her comments. Really listen to his or her feedback and gain valuable insights from his or her perceptions.

❑ Summarize your own situational analysis in the space that follows the example.

Sample Situational Analysis

The owners of a small business conducted a S.W.O.T. analysis to assess why complaints from their three key customers had increased. Their abbreviated situational analysis included:

- *Strength:* We provide generally good service, creating a solid customer base.
- *Weakness:* The inability of our internal systems and manpower to handle growth properly.
- *Opportunity:* To serve our three most important customers with consistent excellence, thus regaining their trust.
- *Threat:* Growing too fast.
- *Lessons learned, or our plan to improve our services:* We've spread ourselves too thin by expanding services too quickly. We need to eliminate, at least temporarily, all non-core services. Once we've regained consistent excellence in our core services, we will discuss and analyze the potential addition of non-core services, one at a time.

MY SITUATIONAL ANALYSIS

Strength: ....

Weakness: ....

Opportunity: ....

Threat: ....

Lessons learned: ....

2. Your Vision

A vision is a picture of the future in its ideal state. I believe God has a clear vision of success for each of us—the problem lies in our inability to see it. Our lives are so immersed in the forest of our circumstances, fears, doubts, and egos; we can never rise above the tree line to see the vision. Instead, we look for signs and miracles from a mountaintop experience to help us see God's plan. In reality, God works the opposite way. As we grow closer to God, He reveals His plan to us, not in its entirety, but in small pieces. It's okay if you're struggling to find a clear vision. Many of us have driven on a desert highway toward a mountain range. At first, the mountains appear fuzzy. The closer we get, the more clearly defined the mountain range becomes. Quiet your soul to hear God's voice and see His clues. Act on those clues, one by one, and the vision will slowly become clearer.

THOUGHT-PROVOKING QUESTIONS

Review your situational analysis. What clues do you think God is giving you that could be transformed into a future calling or vision?

....

What would this vision or calling look like?

....

Think back on your daydreams. Describe them. Can you glean a vision from your daydreams?

....

What would you do if you could not fail? Could this be part of your vision?

....

What would you do if money was no object?

....

ACTION PLAN

☐ Read the Book of Nehemiah. Identify three lessons you can learn from Nehemiah's vision.

☐ In twenty-five words or less, write out your vision statement, or try drawing your vision.

An Example Vision

Business people recognize and embrace Biblically based leadership as a credible, viable, and important alternative to other leadership approaches within mainstream corporate America.

3. Your Core Values and Principles

Each of us has a unique set of values and experiences that make up our character. We also have a set of principles that we believe and live by. These values and principles help create our standards of conduct and drive our business decisions. When we live according to them, integrity, personal satisfaction, and fulfillment occur. When we compromise them, we lose our integrity and our personal fulfillment. Therefore, it's important to identify our core values and principles since they not only define how we do business, but they also act as the anchors that ground our decision-making process.

THOUGHT-PROVOKING QUESTIONS

What are the core values and principles that drive your business decisions?

....

What three values and principles are most important to you?

....

Put your values and principles to the test. Which of them would you classify as "non-negotiable"? In other words, what values and principles will you not compromise even in the face of negative consequences?

....

ACTION PLAN

❑ Using the following criteria, create a brief values and principles statement:

- **Approach:** These are the principles and values that describe how you approach your business.
- **Alignment:** Your actions and decisions align with your core values and principles, and your core values and principles align with God's will.
- **Anchor:** These values are the standards of your business decisions.

❑ Once you have your values and principles statement, follow this three-step action plan:

1. Prioritize your top three values and principles using the following criteria:
   - Does it honor God?
   - Does it contribute value?
2. Align your actions with your values.
   - Ask a diverse group of people (family, coworkers, clients, friends, etc.) to describe you. Do their views of you reflect your values statement?
   - Review all the activities you perform in a typical day. Do your activities and actions align with your values and principles?

3. Identify inconsistencies in your actions and develop a plan to eliminate them. Your efforts in this step will further align your actions with your values.

An Example of Core Values and Principles

- Honor the Lord in everything I do, delivering excellence as an ambassador of Jesus Christ.
- Communicate the Gospel in a wise, appropriate, yet bold way.
- Respect diversity in the workplace; providing dignity and worth to all people.

MY CORE VALUES AND PRINCIPLES

....

....

....

4. Your Mission

A mission explains why you do what you do. It provides a succinct purpose or reason for being. When Jesus Christ comes into our life, we begin to understand that we have been called according to His purpose. As Romans 8:28 states, "And we know that in all things God works for the good of those who love Him, who have been called according to His purpose." God has uniquely designed each of us to serve a distinct purpose. He has given us a unique set of talents, gifts, skills, and passions. One of our roles is to discover these special gifts so we can be of greatest service to the Lord and others. By discovering your mission, you help define who you are and how you can best contribute your services to others.

THOUGHT-PROVOKING QUESTIONS

What are you most passionate about?

....

If you were financially independent and money wasn't a significant factor in your decisions, where would you invest your time and effort?

....

Professionally, what do you enjoy doing most?

....

What do you think are your greatest talents and gifts?

....

Think back on the comments and feedback you've received from friends, family, peers, and those in supervisory roles. What common themes regarding your traits and characteristics usually surface?

....

ACTION PLAN

❏ Write your personal mission statement. It should be twenty-five words or fewer and describe how God has designed you to serve His purpose. Don't get caught up in making your mission statement perfect. Instead, focus on what's in your heart. An effective mission statement incorporates your passion, the need you're addressing, the market you're impacting, and your desired outcome. Try to include each of these.

❏ Name at least three actions you can take immediately to start making your mission statement a reality.

An Example of a Mission Statement

Encourage and equip business people to integrate their work and faith, in order to become the success God intended them to be.

YOUR MISSION

....

....

....

5. The Need

At the core of the free enterprise system is the law of supply and demand. In its simplest form, this law states that a successful business determines a need, and then it provides a product or service to fulfill this need. In the same way God calls us to uniquely serve in some capacity, I believe that God uniquely places us to fulfill a distinct need. The more we grow in our relationship with the Lord, the more in tune we become to the needs of others. A significant part of finding your calling is discovering the need you are to fulfill. This will become your focal point, whether it entails fine-tuning your role in your current professional position, finding a new job, starting a business, or enhancing your ministry.

THOUGHT-PROVOKING QUESTIONS

Looking around you, what are the greatest needs you see in your work, in the marketplace, in your community, and in your family?

....

Which of these needs stirs your heart the most?

....

ACTION PLAN

❑ Survey your customers:
- Identify their needs and issues.
- Identify the key obstacles to their success.

❑ There are several ways to survey your customers, including: written surveys, telephone surveys, and personal one-on-one interviews. One-on-one interviews provide the best way to understand your customers. Choose whatever method or combination of methods that work for you.

❑ When looking for the need, seek the LORD.
- **L**isten to understand others more deeply.
- **O**bserve the behaviors of others around you.
- **R**eflect on what you have seen and observed.
- **D**iscern the underlying need.

❑ Make a plan to continue learning about your customers. Just as people and circumstances continually change, so do needs.

❑ In the space below, define the need your product or service will meet.

An Example of a Defined Need

As a management consultant working in the trenches of corporate America, I've observed that it's lonely at the top; it's lonely in the middle; and it's lonely at the bottom. From CEO to line employee, people struggle alone with difficult moral, ethical, and spiritual dilemmas. There are few Biblically based leadership resources to equip and encourage business people to do the right thing.

(Note: This defined need, identified by facilitating executive retreats, doing one-on-one coaching, and conducting surveys, drove me to write God Is My CEO.*)*

YOUR DEFINED NEED

....

....

....

6. Your Unique Quality

Daily, we're pursued by companies trying to sell us everything from weight loss to financial independence. As a result, even when we have something valuable to offer, it's difficult to get our customers' attention. Therefore, we need to find our unique competitive advantages in order to succeed in a crowded and competitive world. Whether starting a business, looking for a job, writing a book, or pursuing excellence in a corporate environment, it's important to discover what makes you different. God created you as a masterpiece ("For we are God's workmanship, created in Christ Jesus to do good works, which God prepared in advance for us to do."—Ephesians 2:10). You have been uniquely designed with your set of talents, skills, and experiences to serve others in a significant and powerful way.

THOUGHT-PROVOKING QUESTIONS

Review your skills, talents, and past experiences. What makes you uniquely qualified to fulfill the needs of your target market?

....

ACTION PLAN

❏ As you grow in character through experiences, God gives you power or authority to aid others in similar situations. As you review your past experiences, identify what gives you the authority to help other people. In the space following the example, describe your unique quality.

An Example of Unique Quality

I was a business executive whose god was the bottom line. My testimony, which includes being fired and finding a personal relationship with Jesus Christ, resonates with people. My business background, my skills as a speaker and consultant, and my faith make me uniquely qualified to speak to business executives searching for more meaning and purpose in the marketplace.

YOUR UNIQUE QUALITY

....

....

....

7. The Target Market

I know many wonderful people who have tremendous hearts for service. Unfortunately, some of them are so scattered in their approach that they wind up being of little help to anyone. In today's busy environment, focus is a key component of success. Now it's time to focus your identified need into a specific target market or primary customer.

THOUGHT-PROVOKING QUESTIONS

Who is/are your primary customer(s)?

....

Who is the person or group of people you want to help?

....

What are their specific needs?

....

ACTION PLAN

- ❏ **Micro view:** Picture the one person with a specific need or struggle whom you can help. Visualize all aspects of that person's dilemma. What's their situation? What pain are they feeling? What kind of help do they need?
- ❏ **Macro view:** Review your customer surveys and identify common needs and issues.
- ❏ As briefly as possible, describe your target market.

An Example of a Target Market

When I was writing *God Is My CEO*, I identified two groups who comprised my target market: (1) The Christian business person who seeks to integrate his or her work and faith in a diverse work environment, but who needs guidance and support to make it happen; and (2) the spiritual seeker (one who does not have a relationship with Jesus Christ) who struggles in business and is searching for meaning and purpose in his or her life.

YOUR TARGET MARKET

....

....

....

8. An Environment for Growth

Part of my personal plan includes membership in a masters swim program. It's a great cardiovascular workout and I know it's an important part of my long-term health. There are days, however, when I'm not motivated enough to go through another demanding workout. What keeps me going is a team that sets me up for success: a swim coach who pushes me to excel and a swim partner who creates a standard of excellence. My swim partner, Rick, never judges me, but always sets a standard of performance that challenges me. These two people have created an environment that brings out the best in me.

Professionally, you need to find an environment that brings out the best in you. You can spend weeks developing a solid business plan, but if you're in the wrong place, it will be difficult to ever realize your plans and dreams. Like the tree planted by streams of living water, you need to be planted where you can grow, mature, and bear fruit.

THOUGHT-PROVOKING QUESTIONS

Does your present work environment allow you to fully utilize your talents, gifts, and skills?

....

Do the people you work with bring out the best in you, or do they stifle your growth?

....

In what kind of environment do you work most effectively? With what types of people do you work most effectively?

....

In what ways can you improve your present work environment?

....

If you lead others (whether formally or informally), how can you create an environment that brings out the best in people?

....

ACTION PLAN

❑ Create your ideal work environment, one that will encourage your growth. Using a blank piece of paper, write or draw a picture of your ideal. Make sure you include each of the following elements:

  • The people you work with (leadership, coworkers, customers, shareholders, etc.)
  • The physical workspace (office conditions, indoors vs. outdoors, office vs. home, etc.)
  • The culture (creativity level, individual vs. team atmosphere, laid-back vs. fast-paced, etc.)
  • The values (the standards and principles that make up the culture)

❑ Once you've identified your ideal environment, choose a course of action to fit your present situation:

  • Remodel your present "home." If you enjoy your present work environment overall but need to make it work better for you, take action. For example, improve your relationship with your coworkers, buy a better desk, personalize your corporate office, or create a dedicated office in your home.
  • Look for a new "home." If your present environment is not conducive to growth and cannot be "remodeled," it may be best to find a new work environment.

❑ If you are searching for a new job, be sure to find a work environment in which you can truly flourish.

❏ If you're working with a specific customer but not getting any satisfaction from your job, look for a target market that will appreciate your services.

An Example of an Ideal Work Environment

People
- Leadership—high moral and ethical standards; hands-off but available as a resource; challenge my thinking; provide constructive feedback
- Coworkers—effective at independent work but present projects as a team; high moral and ethical standards; equal opportunity; exhibit strong work/family balance; good sense of humor
- Clients—provide challenging work that stretches my abilities; give constructive feedback following project presentation

Workspace
- Office or cubicle in a professional office setting, situated near bright, natural light; downtown location within walking distance of bus line and restaurants

Culture
- Fast-paced during the day, but working after hours/weekends is the exception rather than the rule; creativity in working with clients is encouraged and rewarded; professionals do much work independently, but work in teams on client assignments; leadership is highly visible

Values
- Clients come first; any good idea that meets the client's needs is supported; employees are valued, as shown by regular feedback and rewards

YOUR ENVIRONMENT FOR GROWTH

....

....

....

9. Your Products and Services

One of the first sales concepts I learned was the difference between features and benefits. A feature is a fact describing the product or service being sold. A benefit, on the other hand, is a description of how the customer will benefit from or be helped by the product or service. A good salesperson communicates beyond a product's features and explains how the product or service will help or benefit the customer. Regardless of your professional position, a key to your success is to create features that benefit your primary customer. (Remember, your customer may be someone within your company or outside of it. Most of us have multiple customers, including the person we report to.)

THOUGHT-PROVOKING QUESTIONS

Review your unique talents, skills, and experiences with the needs of the marketplace in mind. What product or service do you offer your primary customer?

....

How does your customer(s) benefit from your product or service?

....

ACTION PLAN

❑ After you've answered the previous questions, review the first eight components of your personal business plan.

❑ Through the eyes of your customers, create the ideal product or service.

- If your product or service already exists, identify three actions you can take to improve on it.
- If you are designing a new product or service, partner with a key customer to help you create it.

❑ Describe your new and improved product or service in twenty-five words or fewer.

An Example of Products and Services

Speaking
- Keynote addresses
- Half-day programs
- One-day programs
- Weekend retreats

Facilitating
- Partnering sessions
- Strategic planning sessions

Coaching
- Executive coaching
- Leadership development

YOUR PRODUCTS AND SERVICES

....

....

....

10. Your Strategic Partnerships

While walking through a living room area, the manager of an assisted living facility came upon an elderly woman working on a 1,500-piece puzzle. "I bet it's difficult not seeing the picture among all these pieces," he said in passing. The woman looked up and smiled, responding, "Oh, no. I like it when different people come up and help me by putting pieces of the puzzle together." Sooner or later, we discover that God blesses us through people. He's constantly bringing people into our lives to help us fulfill His purpose. We don't fulfill God's vision, mission, and purpose for our lives in a vacuum—we're part of a team bigger than ourselves. Strategic partners range from close friends to informal advisory boards of trusted peers, to business partners who share your values. Regardless of the formality of the relationships, it's important to make meaningful connections with people who will help you and your plan succeed.

THOUGHT-PROVOKING QUESTIONS
What people or organizations has the Lord placed in your path? Are any of these potential partners?

....

Look inside your marketplace, including your competitors. What people or organizations share your values and passions? Are any of these potential partners?

....

What types of strategic partnerships would support your close personal relationships at home and work? Could your pastor or best friend be a partner in supporting your marriage through rough times? Could your child's favorite teacher provide insights on how you can encourage your child's learning? Could you volunteer for a committee or mentoring relationship at work, one that would enhance your work environment and encourage someone new in his or her career?

....

ACTION PLAN

☐ Identify potential partners who will help you achieve your personal business plan.
  - While it is beneficial to seek people who share your values, don't look for people just like you. There's great strength in diversity. Seek partners who think differently from you, who can support you as well as challenge you.
  - Take considerable time finding the right partners. Mutual understanding, respect, and trust are essential in a good partnership or team.

☐ Schedule a one-on-one partnership meeting where you will develop a mutually beneficial relationship, using the following guidelines:
  - **Perspective:** Develop a mutual understanding of how you and your partner can benefit from this relationship.

Discuss each other's respective strengths, weaknesses, gifts, talents, and calling to see how you can best support each other in your endeavors.

- **Purpose:** Develop a shared vision of success and a common purpose for working together.
- **Positions:** Clarify roles, responsibilities, and the expectations you have of each other.
- **Process:** Clarify how you will work together toward your shared vision of success.
- **Prosperity:** Define the fruits of your relationship. What greater good will come from this partnership?

❑ Identify your strategic partnerships below.

An Example of Strategic Partnerships

- John Terhune: To complement my strength in sales and marketing, I will partner with John to provide administration services. Together, we will form a new nonprofit organization. We will use the Five P's model to formally outline our partnership.
- My wife: My wife will be my partner in raising our children and, because of her insights, I will look to her as the lead in this role. She will encourage me as I support our children through their teenage years.
- Pastor Mark: Pastor Mark and his wife will be our marriage mentors. Their way of life and vibrant marriage is our ideal, and we will meet with them quarterly for wisdom and encouragement.
- Jim Alexander: As my spiritual mentor, Jim will meet with me monthly. Jim's role is to help me mature in Christ.

YOUR STRATEGIC PARTNERSHIPS

....

....

....

11. Your Personal, Professional, and Spiritual Development Plan

As previously described, the three principles behind a successful personal business plan are: seeking God's wisdom, growth, and bearing fruit. Ultimately, we bear fruit as we mature—in other words, growing personally, professionally, and spiritually are key elements of the plan. Previously, we discussed determining the needs of the marketplace and offering products and services to meet them. You will likely find that fulfilling those needs will require you to grow professionally. In addition to having the spiritual and personal maturity to be of benefit to others, you need to be in a continual state of professional learning and skill development in order to fulfill those needs.

THOUGHT-PROVOKING QUESTIONS

Read and meditate on Hebrews 5:11–14. How are you growing spiritually?

....

How are you growing in your personal relationships?

....

What core competencies and skills need further development in order to be of greater benefit to your customer or target market?

....

ACTION PLAN

❑ Participate in an ongoing discussion group or Bible study. This is an excellent means for personal, professional, and spiritual development.

❑ Don't use a lack of money as an excuse for neglecting your development. Check out your local library—today's libraries are a great resource, and they're free. Take advantage of the system to create and design your own plan.

❑ Find a mentor and be a mentor. Whether formal or informal, both aspects of a mentoring relationship can promote growth.

❑ If you work for a corporation or organization, ask if there are funds available to help further your professional development.

❑ Summarize your personal, professional, and spiritual development plan below.

An Example of a Personal, Professional, and Spiritual Development Plan

I will form a business discussion group of twelve men. The impact will be:

- **Personally:** Open up and share our personal challenges and gain wisdom from each other's experiences.
- **Professionally:** Discuss the moral and ethical issues we face in business.
- **Spiritually:** Grow deeper in our understanding of God's Word and become spiritually mature.

YOUR PERSONAL, PROFESSIONAL, AND SPIRITUAL DEVELOPMENT PLAN

....

....

....

12. Sales and Marketing Plan

How will you make the world aware of your products and services? If you represent a business, how do you sell your company's services? If you're looking for a job, how are you selling yourself? If you represent a ministry, how do people learn about you?

Whether an individual, for-profit business, or nonprofit organization, it's important to have goals, strategies, objectives, and plans. These will enable you to better organize your thoughts, prioritize your time, and maximize your efforts. Now that you've documented your vision and mission, you now need the strategies, objectives, and action plans that will help you fulfill it. A typical sales and marketing plan would include the following:

- **Vision**
- **Mission**
- **Core Strategies:** Generally three to five strategies or fundamental focuses to achieve the vision and mission
- **Objectives:** Specific and measurable levels of achievement
- **Action Plan:** Detailed plans and activities

THOUGHT-PROVOKING QUESTIONS

How do you want to be positioned and perceived in your marketplace?

....

How are you currently positioned or perceived?

....

What strategies can you utilize to bridge the gap between where you are in your customers' eyes and where you want to be?

....

Do you get caught up in "activity traps"? They're a useless waste of energy. For example, it's not the quantity of sales calls you make that counts; it's the quality of the relationships you develop.

....

Remember, there is no greater sales tool than an excellent product or service. Sales are a natural byproduct of value-added products and services.

....

ACTION PLAN

- ❑ Re-examine the results of your work. Remember, sales are a natural byproduct of excellent products and services.
- ❑ Review your vision and mission. Identify three to five core strategies that will help you achieve them.
- ❑ For each core strategy, identify an action plan to accomplish it.
- ❑ Write the sales and marketing component of your personal business plan.

An Example of a Sales and Marketing Plan

Vision: Business people embrace Biblically based leadership as a credible, viable, and important alternative to other leadership approaches within mainstream corporate America.

Mission: Equip and encourage business people to integrate their work and faith in order to become the success God intended them to be.

Core Strategy: Create a safe, nonthreatening environment in which business people can connect with each other to discuss their toughest moral and ethical dilemmas, as well as their biblical solutions.

Objective: Create a *God Is My CEO* seminar with follow-up leadership discussion groups.

Action Plan: Targeted mailings to local churches and universities to promote *God Is My CEO* seminars and discussion groups. Conduct one-on-one informational interviews with twenty-five local business leaders to better understand their needs. Develop a marketing brochure.

YOUR SALES AND MARKETING PLAN

....

....

....

13. Your Financial Plan

Regularly, I receive calls from people who want to pursue God's calling but don't because they feel financially burdened. I also receive calls from people who say, "The Lord has called me to . . . [insert a great calling]," then jump on the bandwagon without taking responsibility for the financial predicament in which they put themselves, their families, and others.

Neither extreme aligns with God's desire. Taking risks and being financially wise are both part of God's will and plan. Your decisions require that you simultaneously take a leap of faith, trust in God's provision, and consider your fiscal responsibility. We've been called to be good stewards of the resources God has entrusted to us. This means we need to use not only our gifts and talents wisely, but our time and finances as well. Developing a financial plan will allow you to effectively carry out His plan.

THOUGHT-PROVOKING QUESTIONS

What financial resources will my plan require? What is the cost in terms of time and money?

....

If I choose not to volunteer, what is fair and reasonable compensation for my effort?

....

Can I justify my plan financially? If not, what are the risks of pursuing the plan without adequate funding?

....

If the risks are too great, what financial alternatives do I have?

....

ACTION PLAN

❑ Read the parable of the loaned money in Matthew 25:14–31. Meditate on how best to utilize each of the resources (time, money, gifts, and talents) God has given to you in a trustworthy manner.

❑ Develop a simple budget for your personal work plan, including your anticipated revenue or income, and all of your expenses.

❑ As you develop your financial plan, creatively explore options to make your plan more viable. Examples might include cutting expenses, working a second job, volunteering or seeking volunteers, working flexible hours or providing flexible hours for others, and utilizing your company's tuition reimbursement plan.

❑ Summarize your financial plan, both numerically and in words, following the example.

An Example of a Financial Plan

My growing passion is to help inner city youth develop opportunities in business. In order to do this, I would like to reduce my work schedule to 75 percent, or thirty hours a week. With the remaining ten hours, I desire to volunteer my time to City Action Ministries. I cannot, however, afford to dip into my savings and must ensure that my retirement savings continue to build, even on a part-time work schedule.

	Current	Proposed
Annual Salary	$72,000	$54,000[1]
Annual Expenses	$56,000	$46,000[2]
Additional Expenses	N/A	$2,000[3]
Annual Savings	$16,000	$8,000

[1]Salary is reduced to 75 percent of current level.

[2]$10,000 will need to be cut from my current budget. This will come from the elimination of an annual winter vacation ($2,800), a reduced dining out budget ($1,500), drinking office coffee rather than coffee shop coffee ($300), taking the bus to work three days a week (eliminating parking expense of $1,300), keeping my current car an additional 36,000 miles ($1,200 for each of the first three years), reducing annual clothes expense ($400), the reduction of income taxes ($2,000), and being vigilant on all other expenses (such as dry cleaning and the purchase of miscellaneous household supplies and non-necessary items).

[3]Additional expenses anticipated from volunteer work. Includes mileage, additional meals eaten out (some with a mentored youth), and miscellaneous expenses.

While my annual savings rate is cut in half, I can afford to do this for a period of up to five years because of my previously high savings rate. In three years, I will need to conduct another financial analysis. In the meantime, it appears my financial plan will allow me to pursue my vision and my mission to help inner city youth.

YOUR FINANCIAL PLAN

....

....

....

14. The Fruit

God's fruit comes in two forms: the seen and the unseen. The "seen" are the tangible outcomes that result from our efforts. They may be financial success, increased sales, reduced costs, productivity improvements, etc. Tangible results and rewards can be seen, measured, and recorded. They're important because they can calculate and measure the success of our plan. Tangible results, however, are simply a means to a much greater end. They pale in comparison to the significance of spiritual fruit.

In the spiritual realm, results aren't seen and measured; they're unseen and immeasurable. There are dual benefits and significance to spiritual fruit. Inwardly, we experience the fruits of the spirit: love, peace, and joy. These are the natural outcomes of following God and His plan. Outwardly, spiritual fruit plants seeds in others—this is the difference we make as godly leaders. It's the legacy that we leave.

We each have an ego that loves to see results for our efforts. We've grown up in an achievement-oriented society that rewards winning and success. This situation is further complicated by the cultural emphasis on immediate gratification. As much as we would like a quarterly scorecard that provides measures of our success, God's plan is about significance—significance beyond anything we can comprehend and measure.

THOUGHT-PROVOKING QUESTIONS

What tangible outcomes, results, or rewards would you like to see from your plan?

....

In terms of personal and spiritual fulfillment, what spiritual fruit would you like to experience as a result of fulfilling God's plan for your life?

....

In terms of impact on others' lives, what legacy do you want to leave?

....

ACTION PLAN

❏ Using a journal, begin writing regular letters to the Lord. Identify your struggles, plans, and experiences for Him. Lift your requests up to God in prayer. At a later date, go back through your letters to see how He has both listened to you and fulfilled His promises. While you can never see all His blessings, you will see how God's plan is powerfully working in your life.

❏ Identify the seen and unseen fruit you desire in your life.

An Example of the Fruit: The Seen and Unseen

The Seen

- Financially viable and successful business
- Strong marriage
- Positive feedback from client surveys
- Supportive phone calls, letters, and e-mails
- Evidence that I've helped people overcome their dilemmas
- As a peacemaker, I see harmony between two people or departments with previous discord
- Success for other business leaders I've helped
- Children who are godly, have strong marriages, and are successful in God's eyes

The Unseen

- A life filled with joy, and God's peace and love, even in difficult circumstances
- Creation of both disciples and leaders
- Changed lives
- Spiritual maturity
- A legacy that positively influences my family and the lives of those I've touched for generations to come

YOUR FRUIT: THE SEEN AND UNSEEN

....

....

....

15. Renewal

Even youths grow tired and weary, and young men stumble and fall; but those who hope in the Lord will renew their strength. They will soar on wings like eagles, they will run and not grow weary, they will walk and not be faint.

—Isaiah 40:30–31

Imagine being under tremendous pressure and working at a frenetic pace from dawn until early afternoon. You're hungry and tired, but you face an in-basket overflowing with deadlines as well as clients. Your boss, recognizing your dilemma, tells you, "Go, find a quiet place with the Lord and get some rest."

Sound unreal? That's exactly what Jesus tells us to do. "The apostles gathered around Jesus and reported to him all they had done and taught. Then, because so many people were coming and going that they did not even have a chance to eat, he said to them, 'Come with me by yourselves to a quiet place and get some rest.'" (Mark 6:30–31). I conducted a retreat with a group of nurses who cared for their patients with excellence, but were becoming almost ineffective because of burnout. They were taking care of everyone except themselves. Renewal is just as important as any other part of your business plan. You cannot effectively be of service when you're running on an empty tank.

THOUGHT-PROVOKING QUESTIONS

How do you renew yourself spiritually on a daily basis?

....

What do you do to renew yourself weekly?

....

Pull out your calendar. Do you specifically plan time for renewal throughout the year? Read Matthew 11:28–30. What does it mean to "rest in the Lord"?

....

ACTION PLAN

☐ Daily plan: Build in a daily "walk with God." I find taking a walk alone with God every morning gives energy and focus to my work.

☐ Weekly plan: Following the Fourth Commandment, make the Sabbath a day of rest. Set aside one day a week to rest in the Lord.

☐ Annual plan: Renew your business plan annually (quarterly is even more effective). During this renewal process, review the first fourteen components of your personal business plan. Conduct a S.W.O.T. analysis to determine which components need updating: New markets? New products or services? New people? New communication plans? New strategies? Revised vision or mission? New approaches to business? Once your S.W.O.T. is completed, identify specific action items to renew your business.

☐ Summarize your plan for renewal following the example.

An Example of a Plan for Renewal

Renewing daily will help me live one day at a time. Each day, I will schedule three sessions of rest and renewal:

- A "walk with God" every morning
- A transition time between work and family
- Evening prayer before bed

YOUR PLAN FOR RENEWAL

....

....

....

INDEX

ABOUT THE AUTHOR

Larry Julian is a bestselling author, speaker, and executive coach with over two decades of experience helping CEOs, entrepreneurs, and small business owners successfully lead with their faith and values. As a business coach, he helps leaders transcend challenging situations and succeed in the midst of difficulty. His passion is to help business people overcome the dilemmas that keep them from experiencing the success God intended.

Larry is founder of the Leadership Roundtable, a group of senior executives who meet monthly to discuss issues relevant to work, faith, and family. By transforming God's timeless wisdom into daily practical application, Roundtable members are growing and impacting their immediate spheres of influence in a wide range of industries.

Larry's work has been featured in numerous publications, including the *Wall Street Journal*, *Inc.* magazine, CNN.com, and *Fortune*. He's also appeared on *The 700 Club* and *The Tavis Smiley Show*.

In addition to *God Is My CEO*, Larry's business leadership books include *God Is My Coach: A Business Leader's Guide to Finding Clarity in an Uncertain World* and *God Is My Success: Transforming Adversity Into Your Destiny*.

Visit *www.larryjulian.com* for more information.